Little Friends

Asia/Pacific/Perspectives
Series Editor: Mark Selden

Little Friends

Children's Film and Media Culture in China

Stephanie Hemelryk Donald

ROWMAN & LITTLEFIELD PUBLISHERS, INC.
Lanham • *Boulder* • *New York* • *Toronto* • *Oxford*

ROWMAN & LITTLEFIELD PUBLISHERS, INC.

Published in the United States of America
by Rowman & Littlefield Publishers, Inc.
A wholly owned subsidiary of The Rowman & Littlefield Publishing Group, Inc.
4501 Forbes Boulevard, Suite 200, Lanham, Maryland 20706
www.rowmanlittlefield.com

P.O. Box 317, Oxford OX2 9RU, UK

British Library Cataloguing in Publication Information Available

Library of Congress Cataloging-in-Publication Data

Donald, Stephanie.
  Little friends : children's film and media culture in China / Stephanie Hemelryk
Donald.
    p. cm. — (Asia/Pacific/Perspectives)
  Includes bibliographical references and index.
  ISBN 0-7425-2540-6 (alk. paper) — ISBN 0-7425-2541-4 (pbk. : alk. paper)
  1. Mass media and children—China. I. Title. II. Series.
HQ784.M3D66 2005
302.23'083'0951—dc22

                                                                    2005003076

Printed in the United States of America

∞™ The paper used in this publication meets the minimum requirements of
American National Standard for Information Sciences—Permanence of Paper
for Printed Library Materials, ANSI/NISO Z39.48-1992.

This book is dedicated to the little friends from Jiangsu, Shandong, Shanghai, Beijing, and Hubei who drew such lovely pictures to show us what's good about film and TV!

Contents

Preface

This book aims to make a contribution to the growing debates on children and media worldwide. In particular, the book is designed to draw the interests and experiences of Chinese children into the discussion, focusing to a large extent on one medium, film, and one media ecology, education, in the process. It therefore offers extended case studies of personalities, events, and cinematic texts that transect these spheres of attention. Throughout the book attention is paid to the comments of interviewees, whose input has been central to the shaping of the examples, ideas, and analyses offered here.

The book follows the trajectory of contemporary media analysis in privileging the *use* as well as the *content* of media. The "turn" to the end-user provokes discussion of media literacy, cultural competencies, and perhaps especially in the Chinese case, a consideration of the desired uses of media in relation to state priorities and social expectations. This is a trend that belongs to an era of digital experimentation and commercial development in interactive television, streamed news and entertainment, and the multiple unintended uses of Internet and mobile technologies. Notwithstanding the contemporary context, the arguments here look at a range of media deployment, which are not especially new in technological terms, but which evidence new insights into a Chinese media system for children.

The first chapter suggests that, despite continuing fissures across some disciplines, an integrated approach to children's media study is already in train, and that the inclusion of Asian perspectives could only benefit this multidisciplinary field of study. The links between education and psychology are strong, but arguably centred on European and U.S. understandings of the child in society. Media and cultural studies researchers are also cited as leaders in the field, combining observational, industrial, and textual analysis of demographic groups and their social settings. It is hoped here that the insertion of Asian cultural studies methods and interests will add another layer to these types of understanding. Asian studies boasts strong dependencies in language, history, and area specifics. Asian cultural studies (and journals such as *Inter/Asian Cultural Studies, Positions: East Asia Cultures Critique,* and the *International Journal of Cultural Studies* underscore its arrival in the academy) is a field that aims to take on some of those disciplinary responsibilities while also working with ideas spawned in cultural and media studies, and the various disciplines that they encounter, from anthropology to sociology and political science. As a result, the findings of this book are indebted to the studies of state and society that inform so much of modern China scholarship.

In chapter 2, a history of children's film is offered through the memories of leading participants in the industry. Their emotional impact as witnesses to a vibrant and searing period of history lends an affective component to the analysis. This approach privileges a generation of retired media workers whose story is not likely to be picked up in the current rush of new media and new politics, but who are yet vastly important to an articulation of the child's place in the media ecology of China. Their histories are then contrasted with the status of children as consumers in a new economy that mixes the power of money with the intransigence of political control in a fashion quite particular to the modern Chinese state. The contradictions between Western paradigms and those in China are the nub of this contribution to a global discussion of children's media use.

The final chapters explore the nature of media use, media control, and also unexpected usage patterns as they appear in education and in children's accounts of their taste preferences. The interventions of state-sponsored programs are countered with the imaginative applications of both children and their teachers. While innovators might also pursue very fixed notions of child development, there is still a sense that their innovations inadvertently support direct negotiation between children and the media they encounter and use through their schooling at primary, secondary, and tertiary levels.

The final chapter argues for a nuance in the association between national style, patriotic media attention, and globalizing media cultures. The argument posits a theory of cosmopolitanism as a mutated version of national taste structures, presenting the complex and inventive ways in which children deal with unfamiliar cultural contexts on screen. The last chapter has been influenced by my involvement in a project looking (in part) at the degree to which the fashionable idea of creative activity in the knowledge economy is a travelling strategic concept. That problem is still under investigation, and I suspect will not be answerable for some time, but the overriding contention of this book is not. Children are the mainstay of the present and the future, and their relationship to the economies through which we manage our social and cultural lives must always be a focus for research across the disciplines that ask such questions.

Sydney, 2004

Acknowledgments

Funding and support for the work described here has come from the University of Technology Sydney, Murdoch University, the University of Westminster, the Australian Research Council, and the University of Melbourne. Harriet Evans and Jeffery Wasserstrom were particularly influential in setting me on this line of enquiry thanks to the posters project at Westminster and Indiana in 1997–1998. Fan Wenfang and Sue Ledger helped me find my way into education theory and practice at primary school level—a continuing journey. Yingchi Chu, Zou Luwei, Wang Qian, Leixia Peterson, Jane Sayers, and Bridget Phua have all at various times provided excellent research assistance and advice. Special thanks to Wang Liu-Yi and the Lan Mao Television Co. for access to materials and images and for discussions of the Film Course; to Yu Lan, Lin Amien, Xie Tian, Guang Chunlan, and other workers at the Children's Film Studio in Beijing for their time and hospitality; to all the teachers and students who took part in the Zibo Film Conference; and to the hundreds of students, parents, and teachers who have filled out questionnaires for me over four years, who have answered interminable queries on their media tastes, have drawn beautiful pictures, and have watched very old films on my behalf. The young people who have taken part in focus groups have truly been little friends (*xiao pengyou*) and very patient ones. Thanks also to Morag and Ellen Donald for their help in the playground, classroom, and in Children's Day research, to Brogan Bunt, Ingrid Richardson, Sheng Anfeng, Wang Ning, and Andrea Witcomb for their involvement in the Western Australian and CD-ROM stages of the project, and to Michael Keane for his support as a constant co-worker in the Asian media project in Australia. I also owe thanks to Tim Wright, Tom O'Regan, Gail Phillips, and Alec McHoul at Murdoch, to Ken Gelder and Simon During at Melbourne, to Yin Hong at Tsinghua, and to Yingjie Guo at UTS, who have all in various ways supported the research that made this possible. Finally, I would like to thank all the students and teachers at Murdoch University who have found children's media interesting, especially Jane Stadler and Kathleen Baldwin.

Some of the work contained here has been developed through other media-centered discussions. These publications include: "History, Entertainment, Education and Jiaoyu: A Western Australian Perspective on Australian Children's Media, and Some Chinese Alternatives," *International Journal of Cultural Studies* 4, no. 3 (2001): 279–99; "Children's Day: The Fashionable Performance of Modern Citizenship in China," in *Fashioning the Body Politic: Dress, Gender and Citizenship*, ed. Wendy Parkins (Oxford: Berg, 2002), 205–16; "Women, Technology in the Teaching Profession: Multi-literacy and Curriculum Impact" in *Chinese Women: Living and Working*, ed. Anne McLaren (London: Routledge-Curzon, 2004), 131–46; and "The English Project: Function and Culture in New Media Research" (with Ingrid Richardson), *Inter/Sections: The Journal of Global Communications and Culture* (2003). Seminars and meetings on children's media and literature in China (organized by Andrew Jones at Berkeley), on political communications in the PRC (organized by Maurizio Marinelli at the AAS, 2002), on gendered Internet use (organized through UTS and the University of South Australia), and on the economy and creative industries (organized by John Hartley at QUT) have also been very helpful. The emphasis taken here is rather different from these previous discussions, but I am nonetheless indebted to coauthors, editors, and seminar leaders for ideas that have emerged from our work.

The book is published by Rowman & Littlefield, under the editorship of Susan McEachern. I would like to thank Susan for her ongoing commitment to Asian scholarship and to the importance of children in all our thinking. Mark Selden is a series editor of formidable scholarship and logic, and I greatly appreciate his time and efforts here. Thanks to Karen Hasin-Bromley for her skilled eye in the preparation of the manuscript. I also owe thanks to authors whose novels I read during the writing of this book including Saskia Beudel, Barbara Patterson, and especially Philip Pullman whose trilogy, His Dark Materials, clears a space for children and adults and those who want to write about ourselves in both capacities. The greatest debt is to James Donald for reminding me about literature and for the cottage in Augusta with thanks for his love and support in some difficult times.

This book is dedicated to Sallie Westwood and Harriet Evans: wonderful role models.

1

Children's Media Research in an Asian Studies Context

In the 1980s, critics and scholars in the West "discovered" Chinese film. Many were concerned to give airtime to the new directors, cinematographers, and writers of the Fifth Generation, while others delved deeply into the antecedents to the new talents who emerged from the Beijing Film Academy in 1984 (Berry and Ni Zhen 2003). They discovered a history of melodrama, social realism, revolutionary romanticism, and—above all—"type." Paul Clark's typologies of revolutionary stories (Clark 1989) were illuminating: the soldier hero, the dubious and garrulous old woman, the eager female recruit, the old man faithful to a ruined order of feudal privilege, but finally redeemed, and the irredeemable traitor. In the years since those books were published, another type has come to my attention. This is the young boy: naughty, passionate, and brave. He has travelled through children's film from Sanmao the Ragged Shanghai Street Urchin *(1949) to* Little Soldier Zhangga *(1963), and latterly to the fish-boy in* I Am a Fish *(2002), desperately swimming to find his grandfather in the open sea. He also exists in animation,* Nuzha Calms the Sea *(1979), as Monkey King, the classic trickster hero, in* Journey to the West *(2000), and, in* Lotus Lantern, *falling into the vortex to rescue his mother from an evil magician uncle (2001). And still, in 2002 in a small town hotel in dusty Zibo in the northern province Shandong, a schoolboy draws Sanmao in answer to the question: what do animation and live action drama mean to you?*

CHILDREN'S MEDIA STUDIES

Children's media communications studies comprise a field boasting a range of scholarship, methodological interests and institutional homes. Its origins lie somewhere between psychology, education, and public information (Ashbach 1994; Li 2002), but its current expressions are found in media and cultural studies, psychology, education, and—to a lesser extent—social anthropology (Allen 1994). The most studied medium is television, with computer technology and classroom media also well documented. Radio is understudied, and children's film tends to only emerge in cultural analyses of Disney or in historical accounts of animation (Curtis 1995). Advertising and merchandising are often mentioned as worrying sites of child exploitation and a way in which children are wooed into the economy of consumption and market-led values endemic in Western societies (Murdock and Zhao 1995). There are few English-language studies of children's media outside the dominant mainstream Anglo cultures of the United States and the United Kingdom, although Unesco reports are international in scope (2000; 2002).

International studies that are emerging in the Asia-Pacific and India tend to come from mass communications experts. This small but growing interest in children is also evident among Asian studies scholars, and hopefully they, and their students, will read this book as a bridge between the disciplines. To that end, some media studies terms are explained in detail, to ensure that all readers have a fair chance of evaluating the material here. Likewise, some elementary facets of Chinese studies are rehearsed for the benefit of readers coming from a different location and perspective. Wherever possible, examples are used to develop the conceptual contentions of the discussions, and illustrations are included to allow readers some sense of the media objects in question. As with many historical documents, these are not easily available, and it is hoped that illustrations accord at least imaginative access.

The emphasis in this book is on film, with discussion also of television, and human-computer interaction. Film is just one starting point for studying the mass media in China, but it is a passionate medium, provoking strong reactions from audiences, practitioners and bodies of authority. As such, it works well as an entrée into the mediated world of China's young generations and their parents. Much of the fieldwork took place in and around the school system (see notes on method in the appendix), so there is a bias towards children's media as used and understood in relation to that particular context. This set of interests takes the book a little away from children's media study as it is most often conceived, as a study of television. This in turn moves the work away from the discussion of cause and effect that is a significant motivation behind many studies of that medium. How many times has the other great communicative system, the print media, blamed television for child-on-child violence, for domestic disharmony, and for the sad new world of the couch potato? This book does not go down that path.

That said, there is a strong dependency here on some ideas that have grown out of thinking to do with television, and its associated medium of advertising. In studies of television there is a continuing media-psychology school, with an emphasis on effects, particularly in relation to marketing, branding, and consumption. Media effects theory is not the main interest of this book, but one approach to thinking about the effects of media is very important here, and this is the educationalists' idea of media literacy. Media literacy can be used as a measure of children's grasp of visual communications, or technical skills and of multistrand storytelling. Here it is understood as a measure of the intelligence and knowledge that children bring to bear on their media use. Recent work in Taiwan of this type is Wu Chih-hsien's study of the effects of advertising on young people in Taiwan. Wu concludes that, whilst behavioural outcomes from viewing advertisements were not clearly measurable, it was nonetheless arguable that media literacy programs would assist young people in dealing with the associative and branding techniques used by the advertising industry (Wu and Chou 2000). Wu has also argued that children's consumption of Japanese animation is similarly dictated by fashion rather than an intrinsic relationship with a particular show or set of characters, or, as a film scholar might argue, the audience's identification is with the genre not any one particular example (Wu C.-H. 2002).

Media literacy is a practical tool for children in Wu's analysis, and a signifier of children's agency in media use in my own work, but it is also a key theoretical term in children's media study as it provides a link between different disciplinary approaches. Literacy refers to learnt access and an associated degree of creative skill within a particular communication system, usually a written language. In the present era, literacy has been conceptually expanded to include the use of computer-based communications, and to encompass the notion of visual literacy, which feeds a wider idea of media literacy. Visual literacy is a term that metaphorically accords some status to the way in which people understand visual communications (pictures, film, television, websites and—before mass literacy—stained glass windows!), but can also infer that the "literate" have the skills to produce, or at least understand the technical construction of, such communicative methods and sign systems. Hence film "language" is increasingly taught in secondary school systems in some parts of the world, as part of a move to acknowledge the actual literacies required in modern everyday life and in the contemporary workforce. Even in China, where the education system is well renowned for conservative tendencies, there are national moves towards computer competencies at secondary and tertiary levels, and a pilot "film program" is running in several provinces (see chapter 4). It is important to be clear, however, that media literacy is a term that depends on its ideological context for clarity, and also on its linguistic and cultural domains. Filmmakers in 1960s Japan did not use the same grammatical "codes" (Burch 1979) and certainly not the same technologies of film practice as did their colleagues in China in the 1950s and practitioners in Hollywood in the 1990s. Viewers of *The Matrix*

Reloaded (2003) are assumed to be literate in games technologies as well as in cinematic storytelling. Literacy is not free-floating. It is embedded in the daily realities and possibilities of its deployment. In a tertiary domain in an Australian or U.S. university, critical and creative thinking might well be assumed within the ideal media literacy, whereas in a Chinese secondary school that expectation is unlikely and probably deemed undesirable.

"Literacy" as a research idea and applied concept therefore nicely brings together psychology, media studies, education, and social anthropology: literacy articulates the developmental system of psychology, the possibilities of educational intervention, the importance of media in the contemporary world for all audience members, and the understanding of sociocultural-technical environments which determine markers of learning and status. Media literacy programs in the United Kingdom, France, and Australia, at secondary and tertiary levels, emphasise the deconstruction of programming content, by teaching the grammatical patterns of film and television language, and allowing students to discover the creative potential of the media. Similarly, any computer-based education that allows children to understand programming techniques, simultaneously gives them intellectual access to the ways in which content has been prepared for consumption.

But, as I have suggested, media literacy does not necessarily include a critical edge to the use and understanding of a communicative system. That can only be derived from an educational environment that values and encourages independent and argumentative thought. The content of a medium is produced through complex sociocultural and ideologically manipulated processes that cannot be swept aside by techno-grammatical competency (although, arguably, they cannot be examined without such competency either). In China's Film Program described later in this book there are many films (over five hundred) available to study, but only those five hundred are permissible in the classroom. Middle class urban children with some money to spend can see illegal (or legal) copies of other material and make their own comparisons, and then their literacy has expanded its potential. If they are rural or small town children whose parents are spending every spare cent on their schooling, then they are probably restricted to what is available through school, and for them literacy is—at least in the short term—giving access to a closed system of meaning and interpretation.

This contention is a real one for children in China, with vastly different levels of income and opportunity (Khan and Riskin 2001), but the uses of literacy provoke heated debate elsewhere in the field of children's media, as there is little agreement on the levels of autonomy possible in a child's thinking. Where psychology, media studies, and education especially tend to diverge is in assessments of children's ability to read media critically based on their own life observations and on their competencies in the particular technology. Some of the arguments underlying this central bone of contention are rehearsed in the chapters here, insofar as they relate to case studies of media usage and child reactions to particular content.

For example, a seven-year-old child who loves Japanese cartoons on CCTV (Chinese Central Television) insists that they are Chinese-made and patriotic (Beijing interview 2000). As researchers we could read her response as (a) media illiterate because she has not yet delineated between Chinese and Japanese animation styles, and has not realised that dubbing is common in imported animation (other children in the same focus group knew this); or (b) that her sociocultural education at home and school prepares her for positive responses to national content, and for unfavourable views of Japan. She therefore equates pleasure with China, and quite logically "reads" a good cartoon as Chinese; or (c) that Japanese cartoons are part of a seductive globalizing trend that misinforms national and local audiences and confuses cultural sensitivities in the young. I would opt for a balanced reading between a and b and would also put that in the context of other children's knowledge, and the lack of media discussion at that school for that age group. I would also be interested to examine the depth of patriotism assumed in the Chinese education system's definition of a well-rounded child's moral "quality" (*suzhi*).

This demonstrates a reasonable helpful dialectic between developmental psychology, educational, and media studies approaches to the child audience. That is, that there is limited agency available to children through media (and cultural) literacy, which works in a context of available content, educational praxis, and market-led or governmentally inspired briefs to the media. The degree to which this literacy facilitates or influences choices and attitudes, whether commercial or political, is always of interest to these areas of enquiry.

Wu's suggestion is that media literacy in Taiwan helps children exposed to alcohol abuse, and the research speaks to the gap that exists between those who see children as a blank slate on which the media scrawl their influence, and those who see children as active and potentially creative consumers of media product. This argument has long-term political ramifications for children. In one version of reception, they are characterised as wards of the adult symbolic world, always vulnerable to manipulation and victimisation by their elders, and always, by implication, subject to the norms prescribed by those who measure the "effects" of media influence. On the other end of the argument, there is a version of children as creative agents in a world organised through consumption and mediated communications. This account allows that children are part of society and that they must therefore have rights, subjective meaning, and effects of their own. This argument may also, however, play into the notion that a closed circle of consumption is not only necessarily desirable but is also the only form of "creative" meaning-making available to young people in a globalizing mediated economy. This is a trap that I believe I fell into in an earlier iteration of this work when discussing internationalisation, and would certainly withdraw it now (Donald 2004, 52). The point of media literacy is simply that it should assist children to articulate their place in the world through those media and educational opportunities available to them.

On this trajectory, strategic arguments may be deployed to argue for children as gatekeepers of their own taste culture, and as arbiters of their own cultural boundaries. In the first version children are wards of an adult cultural state, in the second children occupy their own media sphere, and manage their own consumption practices, to the degree supported by their family's wealth, by the social influences of their upbringing, and by the reach of the state. They are therefore active agents in a mediated society, but the society may be more or less open to developing that agency. This debate has not been joined previously in relation to Chinese children, who are assumed to be part of an overall system of controlled consumption and political management. I hope that the arguments and case studies in the following chapters mitigate this position, and suggest a more complex view of children's media use in the PRC.

The leading U.S. children's television analyst Ellen Wartella has recently argued (2002), that those same lines of debate are tending in Western contexts to a more nuanced deployment of either of the extremes I offered above. In my argument I take the line that children are indeed active agents in the media spheres in which they live. They choose and they reject certain products. Where they cannot easily reject a product (as, for example, in the early 1970s in China when there was very little to choose from), they make it their own, play imaginative games with it, and appropriate it for their generation. When thirty Chinese-Australian adults separately recalled *Sparkling Red Star* (*Shanshan hongxing* 1974) and *Little Soldier Zhangga* (*Xiaobing zhangga* 1963) as important films from their youth, they were not necessarily recalling or supporting the absolutely explicit ideological content of these texts.[1] In some cases they may have been nostalgic for the political certainty and competency of a different time and place, but, if so, this was part of a complicated recall of childhood itself. They remembered a figure of the child deployed for adult political ends, but also and nonetheless an intrinsic part of their precious memory of childhood. These memories prioritise the child figure in the films as an agent of a history lived and remembered, rather than as a document of ongoing political will. When first generation Chinese-Australian parents were asked if they would like their children to see the films, they eagerly agreed (about sixty families attended two screening events over two days). On watching the films together with their children, however, they felt that the historical contexts were more specific than they had recalled and that their (Australian) children would not after all appreciate what they had remembered as so redolent of their own youth.[2] In the meantime in Beijing a very senior party executive in his early seventies walked in on a (domestic) private screening of *Shanshan Hongxing* for the researchers. He looked at the film for a couple of minutes and then exclaimed, "I can't watch it, it's so stupid. It was stupid." He left the room abruptly, and then over supper told stories of his humiliation in the late 1960s and early 1970s, the period of the film's genesis and popularity. He had never before communicated these stories to his Australian niece (one of the research team). The film had had an effect, not on his behaviour, but on the passionate extent of his recall. He was still much too close for a nostalgic reading of the text, which was associated with his middle age rather than his childhood.

Chinese-Australian children and Beijing children had mixed reactions to *Shanshan* and *Zhangga*. A few Beijing children had seen Zhangga on CCTV6 (the movie channel which is available on subscription), and they liked the Zhangga character, but weren't very keen on the film itself, "too old-fashioned." The Australian children had not seen it before, and also found it old-fashioned, and did not recognise the boy as the main character. One factor for the children's mixed responses to the films was linguistic. Although "action" excerpts were chosen with very little spoken Chinese content, and although all school-age Australian children in the surveys and focus groups learnt Chinese at Saturday school and spoke it to varying degrees at home, it was not their language of choice. In fact it was a moot point whether any of the children appreciated the films or not. They certainly watched them differently and with an alternative set of media and language literacies to those of their parents.

As has been described elsewhere (Chu, Donald, and Witcomb 2003), the boys in particular were scornful of the fighting skills of the would-be revolutionaries in both *Shanshan Hongxing* and *Little Soldier Zhangga*, whilst one of the older Australian girls deconstructed the use of black and white film stock in a war film (*Zhangga*), arguing that the lack of color indicated poverty in the film system as well as in the diegesis of the film's internal story. Both her assumptions were correct. In the latter case, the girl's advanced media literacy (probably learnt as part of her training for grade 12 English exams) helped her watch the film but did not allow her to understand its historical impact. She answered her questionnaire in Chinese and English, perhaps to demonstrate her literacy to the researchers and to herself. However, despite her obvious cleverness, she admitted to being confused about the historical context of the plot. She did not appear to have been tutored by her parents (or anyone else) on the revolutionary period, or on the 1960s. In fact, none of the Australian children gave any indication of a cultural immersion that had an historical dimension, although their home lives and their parents' immediate history (first generation, post-1985 migrants from the Mainland) might have suggested otherwise. They were enrolled in Saturday language classes but none had absolute language competency in Chinese. On reflection, the researchers recognised that the overwhelming response to our screenings from many ethnic Chinese groups in the state (Mainland, Singaporean, Taiwanese, Malay, and so on) hinted that this offered a convivial and nontraumatic way to start up the children's media education into their parents' pasts.

The "contextual" requirement is perhaps then another aspect of media literacy, a proactive approach to effects, brought about through a synthesis of psychological and educational approaches to the media (see for example, Silverblatt 1995). I would also associate literacy with competency, which avoids a blank slate model of effects, but allows that the competency of children as social actors is a factor in their (positive and negative) negotiations with the media image. These competencies may either be directly applied media literacy skills, or they may be—as the parents suggested—sociocultural (and political) knowledge built on experience in the world.

CATEGORISING CHINESE MEDIA

Literacy provokes and supports competency, and literacy is in itself a competency. Neither determine the manner in which they will be deployed by their bearers, nor the degree to which they will create or maintain creativity and critical responses to existing content. Agency, another concept that blends confusingly with the canon of terms in children's media study, can also indicate a critical and active component of media use, or simply some kind of participation in the process of media choice.

Children's agency is beginning to appear as a strategic category in writings on media within the Chinese academy. The quantitative research comes from the social science background of most writers, who count and tabulate choices and preferences. The results of these counts may not always be illuminating but the fact of counting makes the point that there are countable units (children as part of an audience) out there. The analysis is tangential to the tables but insightful nonetheless. The researchers (who are not named in the report [2000] quoted here but are part of a team at the Chinese Teenage Research Institute) argue that agency is desirable but limited for two reasons. First, children are not catered for as expressive subjects. They are given media content that satisfies adult notions of childhood, and that speaks mainly to the fantasies of childhood that support adult social control. Second, children have little or no input into the development of media content or form. These conditions produce a media diet that emphasises childishness and "prettiness" in all subjects. Examples are not given. An example of this might, however, be the CCTV documentaries on children in the western provinces (1999–2000), a series of short films that presumably contributed to the "opening up the west" (*fang xi*) campaign of the time. The notion of minority peoples' need to be "opened up" to Han leadership and standards is a familiar story of domestic colonisation, and region building (Goodman 2004) managed in part through education policy and practice (Hansen 1999) and in part through infantilisation of the subject (Gladney 1994).

Minority children in documentary films are projected as clever, decorative and different, but their problems (such as poverty, access to media and affordable education) are not foregrounded. Films that deal with minority themes are similar, but there are exceptions. The director, Guang Chunlan, of Xibo nationality herself, has built a career on combining the emotional caché of children with the "prettiness" of minority dance forms, dress and music-making. In *The Drummer of Houyan Mountain* (*Huoyanshan laide gushou* 1991), a boy drummer is "discovered" by the Urumqi Children's Troupe. The story of his experiences outside his homeland relies on the music and dance of the Xinjiang region for its emotional effect. In the end it is hard to remember anything distinctive about the boy's experience beyond a generalised multicultural wash of musicality. In *Feifei Becomes an Actor* (*Feifei cong yingji* 1986) a boy is involved in an acting adventure when a film troupe comes to his village to film an anti-Japanese war drama. This film does not cite the boy's minority status other than through his exclusion from cultural activities enjoyed by some urban children. The researchers referred to above may of course have only been referring to children's television shows which are presented by pretty women, have pretty sets, and do not discuss anything remotely difficult in the children's lives, or in the lives of their fellow children. They were probably also concerned with the lack of programming for teenagers in China, a problem echoed in many media spheres, forcing teenagers to watch children's shows or adult programming, neither of which adequately address the particular challenges of being a young person. However, it should also be noted that children's problems are being recorded on screen, and in an accessible narrative mode that has developed from 1950s and 1960s family film drama into social drama for young people. In these films, there is still a strongly observed aesthetic of childhood beauty and of gorgeous landscapes, but these are not so much pretty as elegiac. Xu Geng's *Thatched Memories* (*Cao fangzi* 2000) records the story of a group of rural school children in 1961. The leading boy is the narrator of the piece, observing the challenges of rural hardship in a period of national famine (although the latter is very understated in the film). Each child performs a parable of modern Chinese experience. The "rich" child, the only one with a bicycle, is reduced to beggary when his father's agricultural business fails. Then, as now, there is little sign of a rural welfare system. The "poor" boy, the clown with the shaven head again reminiscent of Sanmao, resists the disciplines of school but also insists that he should not be left out of teamwork. In the minutes before a school display of callisthenics for local cadres (for a county prize), he grabs the microphone and harangues the school principals—only giving up the podium when he is allowed to perform with the other children.

Surprisingly, in the display he knows all the moves perfectly. However, he does them in reverse, so that he is, perfectly and deliberately, out of sync with his well-schooled fellow students. His display of rebellion is treated lightly in the film. The children think it's hilarious, even the judges are amused, and only the head teacher is distraught as his school loses the callisthenics cup for the first time. But the boy's point is well made. The tall, bald, gangly child seems to be saying: I can also be pretty, but in my own way, and—literally—in my own time.

Although the urge to prettiness in children's media is a politico-aesthetic problem for the researchers, it has other advantages for the outsider. One of the pleasures of talking about media in China with Chinese parents is that they are not overly stressed about levels of violence, nor do journalists assume that American levels of violence in schools will necessarily reproduce themselves in dissimilar societies amongst different cohorts of children in other places, because of shared media. There is a stronger sense of particularity and geographical location than there is, say, in Australia. That particularity is of Chineseness, and is based on an assumption of absolute difference from the developed Anglo societies in the West. This is not to accept that Chineseness is an unproblematic homogeneous concept in media representation, but that, as a non-English speaking country with a strong sense of state power, China does not as yet seem worried that its children's media are drifting towards localised versions of American youth culture and behaviours.

In the developed West, due no doubt to the proliferating relationships and ease of media access between English-speaking countries, children's media are often seen as being on a helpless continuum to the depravity and danger apparently modelled in U.S. social relations. In China, there are instead parental concerns about pornographic tendencies in Japanese animation, about children's decreasing interest in historical subjects, and, as with the social scientists, about the increasing gap between rich and poor, rural and urban children's access to education of any sort, including mediated resources. Japanese animé for children tends to sexualise and elongate the human body. Children are expected to identify with child-women (as in *Sailor Moon*, a popular show about girl-women superheroes, distributed by DIC Entertainment), and their bodies offend Chinese parental and pedagogic sensibilities. U.S. imports are mainly available on VCD, with a few cinema releases (this will, of course, increase as the impact of WTO regulations takes hold) of blockbuster titles, but nowhere near enough to spark real fears of saturation or cultural domination.

Films such as Disney's *The Lion King* are popular with adults and children, and are not cited as a threat in any of our interviews with parents and teachers. Rather, these films are seen as morally upright fables, which suit children's needs and adult agendas. This film tells a universally oriented story of family renewal (the son takes over from the father after a struggle to the death with the usurping uncle, and the rescue of his mother), of the importance of one's native land (despite escaping to a land of plenty the son must return to the ravaged plains of his birth in order to save the land and to take on his inheritance), and of the danger of the Other (in the animated figure of the evil uncle there are definite traces of Semite features, echoing a trend for Arab villains with an English accent in 1990s Hollywood film. If you miss the physiognomy the point is brought home by a hybrid metaphor of Nazism and Islamic symbols: a lion/hyena version of the Nuremberg rallies, which crescendos with a shot of a crescent moon above the floating black mane of the uncle). The deeply racist and Oedipal values at work in this fantasy version of Africa unfortunately sit well with non-Arab, male-centred, family-oriented societies, and China seems to be no exception.

However, these are not issues that are commonly raised in discussions of Disney or of Chinese animation, either in scholarship or by the audience, although such readings would be all too easy to produce. Research on children's media in China cites two major concerns,[3] both of which are peculiar to the Chinese case. First, there is the overriding question of ownership. The media are diversifying and new media groups are emerging as content providers and distributors within the regions. In Shanghai, as the most striking example perhaps, the first distribution company created by a film studio—the East Film and TV Distribution Co. (*Dongfang yingshe faxing gongci*)—was formed in the late 1990s. It combined interests in film, animation, an exhibition chain, and hotels. The Shanghai animation studio is in the fortunate position, apparently, of having strong policy support from the government[4] and an entrepreneurial distribution chain underwriting its access to the domestic markets. In this it is not unlike U.S. studios, which receive strong international support from U.S. government negotiations on GATT (Miller 2002).

Nonetheless, there are only two recent examples of animated film, *Lotus Lantern* (*Baoliandeng* 2000) and the television series *Journey to the West* (*Xi you ji* 1999) challenging foreign (Disney/Pixar) content for popularity. Both these films drew on Chinese style (*minzu shi*) but also adapted Disneyesque animal animation, whilst *Lotus Lantern* was particularly dependent on *Pocahontas* (1995) for its indigenous characters. These films were also notable for extending into merchandising, and thus challenging the creep towards product-driven animation that has taken over in Japan and in the West since the mid-1980s (Pecora 35 and passim).

Some opportunities are lost when studios are either not large enough to sponsor international standard production, or sufficiently well-placed to leverage product enhancement from their industry partners and distributors. *Lotus Lantern* and *Journey to the West* figurines were available, at a high price, in toy stores but did not get distribution through McDonalds or other fast food chains which are usual outlets for Disney tie-ins. Nor has the Chinese games industry yet taken off, so that possible spin-offs in new media technology are not challenging the leaders in that industry (currently South Korea and the United States). These areas of children's entertainment is wide open for exploitation, but only by those who can take on international standards and international merchandising strategies, and beat them on both counts by being more "Chinese." The Beijing-based Film Academy has an excellent animation department, but the Children's Film Studio adventure into digital animation, *Crazy Rabbit* (*Feng tuzi* 2000), did not seem to draw on the talents that should have been available to a state-subsidised studio. The high cost of good digital inserts was cited by a studio official[5] as a reason for the brevity of the computer-animated sequences in the film, but that did not excuse the poor standards of design. Meanwhile, children see Japanese television animation as a standard for "Asian" visual storytelling. Characters from the Hiyao Miyazaki Ghibli Studio are exemplars, for the industry, of quality narration and art direction but also for children's pleasure: Miyazaki's fantastic dream creature Totoro was often mentioned by child interviewees as a favourite.

The second issue is the growing imbalance between rural and urban access to certain media. Computerisation of the curriculum is a reality only in the richer schools, mostly in large cities and along the eastern seaboard. Television penetration is good, but only families with disposable income can back this up with the merchandising that supports a pattern of deep identification with television characters. Also, as Zhong Yong (2003) and others have shown, the television screen is used for multiple entertainment value— from VCDs to karaoke as well as local cable shows and formatted content from larger provincial providers. Chinese-made film for children does not attract high box office percentages, especially at children's prices, and so distribution is done even to the central districts by charity not by government or market.

The Love Children Society (Film and Television Education) (*zhongguo aizi yingshe jiaoyu cujin hui*) was set up specifically to remedy the problems of distribution and to increase awareness of film and television amongst children and parents, and has the support of the studios and the Ministry of Culture. The society's president, Chen Jinti, states that her problems are mainly to do with access, but she is not so much concerned with participation.[6] As I have suggested above, and will argue further in chapter 4, participation is on a continuum with agency, autonomy, and independent deployment of literacy. As such, it is not prioritised by groups with the closest links to government subsidy and to Beijing itself. The Love Children Society falls into this category.

There are, in any case, other, less contentious challenges for rural access. The cost of new media distribution is one. Internet use relies on modems and telephonic or wireless infrastructure. Most remote locations do not have this, and if they do it will be used in educational establishments. Film needs screening, and without the zeal of the old propaganda troupes setting up in remote villages, there is little if any chance of a family cinema being viable in many small towns. Theatres in county towns are self-sustaining and unwilling to run children only shows without subsidy, and the number of viable Chinese screens is falling despite rapid urbanisation (Balnaves, Donald, and Donald 2002). Films for children are occasionally screened on CCTV 6—but this is a channel that needs to be paid for on subscription—so again, rural children tend to miss out. The medium that is cheap and easily broadcast to a mass, and a rural audience, is radio, but this has lost its prime position in the national media sphere. A survey conducted in 1998 and 2000 asked children and parents to name their favourite children's medium. All respondents mentioned television, cinema, computer interaction and about 10 percent also mentioned music.[7] None of the seventy respondents mentioned the radio. Radio is still popular for adults, but television is taking over the domestic realm.

This disappearance of children's radio (at least as far as the audience is concerned) is contested by the national broadcaster. In 1996 People's Radio broadcast a new children's flagship show *Little World* (*Xiaoxiao shijie*), and in 1999 they joined in the seasonal media scheduling with a special show for young people of all minority nationalities on Spring Festival. These efforts are reported in the *Annals of the Children's Century* (2000, 325), but the lack of detail on audience figures and the silence from interviewees suggests that radio in China has not yet reinvented itself as the young persons' communication system strongly linked to music, mobility, and to the Web.

The research categories of children's media in China are familiar: the tussle between local and international content, and the subsequent effects on style; the dominance of televisual technologies with multiple uses and strongly domestic settings; the imbalance in access between the poor and the rich, the geographically marginal and the central, the rural, and the urban, and—affecting all these issues—the economic strictures imposed by modernisation on a developing media economy. Across all these research issues lie the stories that are told to children, why they are told, and what children make of them. Sociality, taught through the education system, and developed in every encounter in the world and in the media sphere, depends on these stories.

MEDIA HISTORIES, CHILDREN'S STORIES

Children's media have been part of the political and social fabric of the last fifty-two years of "new" China. Film, television, and radio have told the national story to a succession of new generations. In recent years, however, the task has been complicated as the story itself begins to contradict the aims and values of the modernising China that provides the contemporary context for this narrative. Perhaps that is one of the reasons for the "prettiness" of children's media, the hard edge of revolutionary narrative has been dulled, and there is nothing strong enough to replace it.

Of all electronic media, Chinese children's film, which emerged in the 1920s, has perforce the longest pedigree. Film has excellent critical credentials from the silent period (1920s–1930s), although most of the supposed classics are not extant. There are also a few classics and many excellent animations from the seventeen years of socialist consolidation, 1949–1966. The animation studios in Shanghai also carry critical value in a received canon of works. Wan Laiming (b. 1899), Wan Guchan (b. 1899), Wan Chaochen (b. 1906), and Te Wei (b. 1915) are four of a number of artists working in animation whose careers have spanned almost a century, and whose work encapsulates the best qualities of Chinese animation national style (*minzu shi*). Each of the three "Wans" uses a different method, drawn animation (*donghua pian*), papercuts (*kezhi pian*), and puppetry (*mu-ou-pian*). These styles are the focus of the shift from hand-laboured artwork to digitised production, the technological end of a modernisation of storytelling. If the change can occur whilst retaining the delicacy of Te Wei's inkwash *Tadpoles Looking for Mother* (*Xiao kedou zhao mama* 1960) and the vigour of Wan Laiming's "Monkey" (Sun Wukung) characterisation in *Trouble in Heaven* (*Danao tian kong* 1960), and the studio's comeback *Nuzha Stirs up the Sea* (*Nuzha naohai* 1979, Shanghai)—then the strength of Chinese animation as a distinct provider of emotional visual narratives might continue.

Radio has also a distinguished, if fading, status in children's media, both for its work as entertainment and as a direct tool of socialisation. In April 1949, Beijing New China Radio broadcast the first child show *A Child's Happy Garden* (*Ertong leyuan*). This was followed by Shanghai People's Broadcasting Company's *The Children's Program* (*Ertong jiemu*) later the same year. Aimed at primary and middle school children, it went out three times a day for twenty minutes, and there was a thirty-minute Sunday special. In the 1960s it was renamed *The Young People's Program* (*Shaonian ertong jiemu*) but in January 1967 the chaos of the Cultural Revolution closed it down. It was relaunched on Children's Day in 1970 as the *Red Soldiers and Young Red Guards Show* (*Dui hong weibing, hong xiaobing guangbo*), but changed back to its previous name on 12 May 1975. If nothing else is remembered from the heyday of children's radio, this one story indicates its precise location within a mediated political landscape, that is at once dedicated to the social importance of the young, but therefore tied to the same political trajectory as everything else.

Radio soldiered on despite the inevitable closedown of media production in the late 1960s. In 1986 the show changed again, not its name this time but its format. It became a magazine show, broadcast six days a week, with items on "Classic Stories," "Letters," "World Music," "Knowledge Palace," and the like. In 1993 the show changed its name for one more revamp *Happy Youth* (*Kuaile shaonian*). It retained the magazine format but emphasised education, and information content. There were many other popular shows in the 1950s and 1960s, mostly produced by People's Radio. In 2002 one of CCTV's 6-100 Projects[8] (*liuge yibai*), a programming initiative for children, celebrated children's storytelling on radio, in particular the contributions of the writer and presenter, Lin Amien. Lin later worked at the Children's Film Studio as a writer and director, embodying a shift of the storyteller and narrative from one medium to the other.

Television for children was pioneered by Beijing Television in September 1958. It had an early focus on child performers, with programs showing children's song and dance routines, *Little Club* (*Xiao xiao jhule bu*) but also drew on the skills of puppeteers with shows like *King Little Hair* (*Wang Xiaomao*) and animators. Each segment lasted about ten minutes. Television shows for children were significant in Chinese television history as their chroniclers claim that they represent the first attempt to target a specific as opposed to a mass audience. Recent media developments, particularly in daytime shows, advertising, and prime time magazine are specifically targeting women, young women, and the thirty to forty age group, respectively. This is a relatively new development in television although the post-1949 print media have always addressed women as a particular child-bearing interest group (Evans 1997).

Television reached several milestones in rapid succession in the early years. In 1958 the first news documentary show for children was produced, *The Start of the New School Year* (*Xinxuenian kaishile*). The idea of documenting the most important day in the year for many children was a good audience pull, and also suggests an understanding of children as actors in the national and social calendar. In the same year, the first full-length drama for children was produced. *The Snow Queen* (*Xue nuwang*) was broadcast on 27 December 1958 by Central Chinese Television (CCTV, *zhongying dianshi tai*). In 1959, the first preschoolers program *Little Friends* (*Xiao pengyou*) recognised the segments within a young people's audience. It went out three nights a week. Its format was not that dissimilar to programs like *Playaway*, *Playschool*, and latterly *Hi-5* that have been the flagships of British and Australian programming. Actors read stories, sang easy songs with educational content, and showed the viewers how to do craftwork; teachers prepared little snippets of information (edutainment); and the artwork of child viewers themselves was highlighted in the program.

Another *Little Friends* show (*Good Little Friends and Books* [*hao pengyou shu*, 1960]) featured famous actors telling stories to groups of children. In later years the actors in these types of magazine shows have become celebrities more for their televisual presence than for earlier film work. In the 1960s, films made people famous, in the 1980s and 1990s films were more likely to be spin-offs from fame built on television work. Celebrity status is peculiar to the television. Radio's Lin Amien had a familiar voice and his stories (which were also published) were beloved by the 1950s and early 1960s generations of listeners, but he is not and never has been a modern celebrity.

Conversely, Dong Huo (b. 1956), the "King of Storytellers" (*Gushi dawang*) started out as an actor in film and television, but made his name as a television storyteller in the 1990s. He is a media celebrity. He appears regularly on "specials," such as the Children's Day Show. In a live performance in 2002, he was greeted with screams of delight when he opened a children's film festival in Shandong with a song and a few jokes. The rise of the media celebrity is a feature of the modernisation and marketisation of children's media. It does not cancel out, however, the overwhelmingly *social* function of national media for children. Thus Dong Huo's appearance in Shandong was in the context of speeches from local Party officials and educationalists, and in the presence of large groups of schoolchildren, rather than children who had attended the event as individual consumers (as might be the case, say, in a U.S. or Australian show starring the Olsen Twins, The Wiggles, and so on).

The position of children in society was in the early years mainly a focus on basic educational and cultural competence. That focus has persisted into the present. At certain moments, however, as with radio and film, a much more explicit engagement with politicisation and socialisation has been evident. In 1976, a 16mm colour special *The Songs and Dances of the Little Red Guards* (*Hongxiaobing yinyue wudiao*) was shot in the south for Beijing Television, presumably at that point as a retrospective. It was the first television show for children shot in full colour. With the introduction of many more provincial broadcasters from the 1980s, children's television has become a more unwieldy commodity. In Jiangsu, for example, an Australian broadcaster delivers revoiced Japanese animation to a provincial market, through a Hong Kong subsidiary. The narrative trajectory of the state, and even of working professionals such as the radio broadcaster Lin Amien, is clearly compromised by this delivery system into the children's media sphere. The eight-hours-a-day programming on CCTV (mainly Channel 7) is shared nationwide, but animations and soaps on local stations are less useful for mass socialisation projects, when scheduling is haphazard, and programming is often randomly bundled with swaps from other stations in other provinces. And, despite calls for intensive production of home-grown animation, production at the state studios is slowing down (dropping from twenty-eight to two reels a year over five years, 1997–2002). This may reflect the growth of independent and coproduction, and suggests that the delivery of "national" content may need to be redefined.

Overall, however, television looks healthy. It enjoys state support and mass popularity. By 2000 China had 640 TV stations broadcasting children's shows. The Ministry of Culture guaranteed in 1995 (through the Six One Hundred projects) that children's programming would remain diverse and committed to children's art forms beyond the popular television magazine format. At the same time, market forces are promoting popular formats in regional and co-productions. As is often the case in China's economy, central initiatives and the regional "pull" contradict but also complement one another. Whether this proves to be for the long-term good or ill of the sector will depend on future regulatory practices, and the degree of sophistication in their balance between commercial freedom, consistent content management, and the direction of the overall national philosophy of media use.

A media use impacting strongly on the children's media sphere is advertising. There is competition for children's attention from a swathe of television advertising for snack foods, vitamins, and toys. In 2000, advertisers spent three times as much on medicine and vitamins promotions as on any other product (Zenith 2002). These adverts are becoming increasingly sophisticated as the market matures, although not as yet as unscrupulous as the fast food and junk food advertising on children's TV in the United States, United Kingdom, and Australia. In 2004, Labour politicians in both of the latter countries have suggested banning these advertisements to cut back on childhood obesity and adult stress in the supermarket. It is unfortunately very probable that similar issues will arise amongst the urban consumers in China over the next few years. Of course, this discussion entails an effects scenario, assuming that advertising "works" and persuades young viewers that they should be eating certain foods because they are fun, cartoonlike—and often indistinguishable from the programming into which they are inserted. Meanwhile, the older methods of poster communications persist in children's spaces (schools, department stores, and play palaces) and latterly video screenings in open spaces (shopping streets and railway stations) are emerging to re-capture a child audience for public communications. These public messages are often especially concerned with environmental issues, which get some thematic attention in Beijing Television's *Big Windmill* (*Dafengche*) and other magazine shows, but which are important enough issues to demand attention across the spectrum of public communications.

It would seem that the nation had prioritised media penetration in an age of many distribution outlets. Yet the vice president of the Love Children Society, Zhu Xiao'ou, admits that in 2002 she has given up trying to serve children outside the immediate reach of the eastern seaboard. Even with sponsorship from the state and from the media industry, her semi-charitable organisation cannot afford to prioritise rural and remote populations. Given that many of the Eastern seaboard provinces already have satellite access to Hong Kong television (Ma 2001), whilst the metropolitan concerns of Shanghai and Beijing grow ever larger with multiple media interests supporting their expansion, the division between the east and the west is opening up in the wrong direction. The situation takes us back to the first concern of Chinese media, the relationship between dynamic production, regulation, and ownership: what, after all, is the benefit of formal and informal state ownership if there is no direct advantage for the large groups in society with poor living standards, and if access to training and talents are not successfully exploited in the industry?

The little urban friends of Chinese media are fortunate in that their access to new media platforms is good, available programming is diversifying, and the special attention paid to them as audience and crucial social sector continues. They increasingly use computer equipment in school and at home, and their access to international content is improving. This should in turn provoke a market-led improvement of quality in terms of production values, but it does not guarantee long-term high quality local product looking at issues and themes particular to the young audiences of modern China, and promises nothing to the rural poor.

The research discussed in this book comprises a series of small studies of a very large population of children in an extremely diverse social environment. Primary research data, film and television texts, creative interactions, and desk research have been brought together to produce a symptomatic reading of children's media culture that refuses an absolute distinction between the "West" and the "East," but which also aims to locate its analysis as a small comment on the manifestation—or not—of global trends in a local context. Where appropriate, therefore, the analysis draws on international perspectives as well as on conditions peculiar to the PRC. The research has been mainly focused on urban contexts and acknowledges that this leaves a great deal to be done on the relationship between a modernising mediated society and those young people who cannot participate in its world. Nonetheless the book does draw on the wider international themes of children's experience in modern and modernising economies. Recent international studies of children and violence, children and agency, children and citizenship, and children as producers of media product are part of the broader theoretical backdrop to the book's argument.[9] The work of cultural historians (Oswell 2002), social psychologists (Clifford, Gunter, and McAleer 1995), media social-economists (Pecora 1998), and marketing specialists (Macklin and Carlson 1999) frames the debates in the United States and Europe. Their models and observations have been taken as reference points in the following chapters. Nancy Pecora's remarks on the long history of children as autonomous consumers are, for example, taken as a useful international context for thinking about the precise nature of recent developments in China. Her account of the socialisation (8) prerogative in branding and advertising in the United States needs in the Chinese case to be understood as only partly exemplified in the less coherently capitalist ideology of a new market economy in a Communist state. Similarly, her summation of the dire consequences of materialism (152–58) are not necessarily applicable to a situation where the integration of political socialisation and media is so strongly supported by regulating institutions. That said, the extended case studies take most of their impetus from the very special situation in modern China at the turn of this century. The descriptive analysis, for example, of The Chinese Children's Film Studio aims to give a snapshot both of the lost ideals of the revolutionary generations (using the key figure Yu Lan as an individualised exemplar of this moment), and a sense of the dynamics and perils of market-led creativity in the face of foreign competition, and in response to children's emerging taste cultures.

A recurring issue is that of education. If there is one indisputable truth about media, children, and China, it is that education is always an imperative in the creation, distribution, and evaluation of media resources for the young. This may be seen in the motivations and justifications for children's programming and film production. It is also evident in the commercial success of new media products. The rising star of English in education has opened up a lucrative field of media production for domestic and institutional consumption. Many of the products available on the market are substandard, and many more are closely tied to the ideological grounds of their originating culture. The Disney Magic English series of VCDs are the clearest case in point. Lessons are structured around songs and stories using Disney characters, and the vocabulary feeds an English world, which can be backed up by feature films, merchandising, and, perhaps in the not too distant future, access to the Disney Channel. It is hard to imagine any child learning usable English from these fast-paced entertainment products, but they certainly enjoy the process. Large urban outlets set aside much more spaces for these educational materials than for any other children's media product except books and comic magazines.

The presence of media is strong in contemporary China and there are proliferating products aimed at the young. Contemporary commentary in the press tends to cover familiar ground in popular media debate worldwide: What are the effects of media on young minds? How does a society endeavour to outline and maintain moral standards and habits of good citizenship? Do the media preserve or corrupt the soul and spirit of the nation? What differentiates the concerns of Chinese parents and educators in the PRC, and those of their Western equivalents? How far may similar themes be understood as truly (rather than semantically) similar? To what extent do the vastly dissimilar political spheres and the experiences associated with accelerated political change underwrite the ways in which we can understand children and media in the PRC? In the following chapter, these questions are addressed through the eyes of media workers whose practice spans the whole of the last fifty years of Chinese political history.

NOTES

1. In questionnaires and focus groups administered in Western Australia in 1999–2000.

2. A full account of this research is given in Donald and Lee (2001) and Chu et al. (2003).

3. China Teenage Research Institution (2000).

4. Television is required to have ten minutes of new domestic animation product as part of its annual broadcast quota. SARFT chief, Tian Congming, was reported by China Media Monitor (2001) to have told the Shanghai Animation Studio that from 2001–2005 the ten minutes a day rule would apply, making 75 percent of broadcast animation "local." Deals to produce local and coproduced animation are regularly reported in the media business lists (usually centred at Shanghai), but there is as yet little evidence of its popular success in children's response to our questionnaires.

5. Interview with Chen Jinti, July 2000.

6. Ibid.

7. Conducted in Beijing by the author, with the assistance of Dr. Yingchi Chu and Wang Qian.

8. The Six One Hundred projects were initiated in 1995 to celebrate children's culture and to encourage new program making. Each program deals with a historical, traditional, or documentary style topic. The Lin Amien retrospective showed contemporary children how radio had dominated mass storytelling in China in the 1950s and 1960s.

9. The study of children's television has a rich history in the United States, in the United Kingdom, and also in Australia. In the United Kingdom there has been seminal work conducted into the child audience and the pros and cons of effects debates (Bazalgette and Buckingham 1995; Barker and Petley 1997; Kline 1993), the child as a subject of education (Walkerdine 1984; 1989) and the child as citizen (Buckingham 2000). The United States has produced a great deal of work based on psychologically modelled research (see for example: Zillman, Bryant, and Huston 1994; Goldstein 1994), but also more culturally oriented examinations of the child in society (Wartella 1979; 1994; Grossberg et al. 1996; Kinder 1998; Spigel 1999). Whilst much of the noted public research associated with Australian children and their experiences with television dates back to the 1970s and 1980s, (Edgar 1977; 1983; 1984; Edgar and Crooke 1976; Hodge and Tripp 1986) there is here too a continuing interest in the subject (Nightingale 2000; Keys 1999), albeit one working in a shifting research environment. In her recent overview of key players in this field, Patricia Gillard maintains that, in an Australian context, there has been a dramatic shift in this area of research in the 1990s reflecting increasing outsourcing of audience research by the state to private companies (Gillard 2002, 78). There continues to be a need for widely conceived and inclusive research into children and the uses of television and related media (Hartley 1998).

2

Film, Family, and Feeling: *Ganqing*

Images of children and children themselves are important for China's secu-
rity. You see, if children are not guided correctly they can easily become
corrupted. Look at me . . . I had no Mother when I was a child. My Father
didn't care about me. I was brought up in a boarding school. But I read a
good many books. I also watched a great many left-wing films in the 1930s.
Twice the town where I was living was lost [captured by Japanese forces.]
Once in Manchuria, and once in Beijing. The second time it happened, in
Beijing, I determined to leave. If I stayed what could I do? Work for the
Japanese? What would that make of me? Who would I be? I'd have become
a housewife [taitai]. (Yu Lan, 1921–, actress and founder, Children's Film
Studio, interview 1999).

This chapter argues that cinema and children's film production in contemporary China offer a glimpse of the ties that persist between revolutionary morality and the future. The observation on which this claim rests is the
striking continuity in the interpolation of *ganqing,* or "warmth of human
feeling" in the films supported and produced by the Children's Film Studio
since 1984. It may not seem surprising that films produced for children
should be about human warmth and kindness. The apparent connection
between revolutionary *ganqing* (the political—not romantic—"feeling" between people of the same class) and the relationships in the Children's Film
Studio films, however, is arguably specific to recent Chinese history. In the
films, the warmth of feeling does not emphasise class feeling, but it is described through the on-screen dependencies of young children and older
people. The director of the studio itself (Yu Lan) and most of the members
of the supporting institution, the Children's Film Society, grew up in the
1920s and 1930s. Their moral outlook was to a significant degree shaped

through the discourses of revolutionary politics and movements of the struggle for Liberation and the foundation of the People's Republic (Ip. 1997). In the 1980s and 1990s, as new generations turned to reform, dissent, and individualistic money-making, and gave up on the morality of class feeling and the collective; these film-makers in turn appropriated the cinematic affections of children, as though that thread of feeling might promote an uncorrupted generation.

In the 1980s and 1990s, a key interpretative issue was to determine the politico-cultural nature and narrational manifestation of "post-socialism" (Dirlik and Zhang 2000; Liu 2004) and post-modernism (Arac 1997). This debate has continued in Chris Berry's work on post-socialism as a theoretical foundation for understanding new documentary (Berry 2002). The broad contention is that socialism is no longer an accurate descriptor for the contemporary Chinese sociopolitical environment, but that, nonetheless, the reforms era has not taken China inexorably into a liberal democratic model of political or social organization. Rather, China is in a seemingly endless period of transformation, and the state is best understood in a metaphor of transition: "post-socialist."

The break with the socialist past, at least as it is expressed in officially sanctioned children's film, is a slowly evolving version of human feeling modelled on the clean lines of revolutionary relationships and carefully managed narratives, combining the best of the very young and of older authority figures. There has been a shift from the intensity of revolutionary stories, but not from the patterns of human relationships at their core. The senior film-workers understand children's film as a key to children's development, and have spent many years working with younger film-makers, to persuade them of the value of talking on film to children. They make an implicit but sharp distinction between the work of television as a mass medium with low aesthetic potential, and film as a theatrical medium with high aesthetic worth. Media aesthetics are then associated with political and moral communicative value. This mode of distinction is a typical disjuncture, which can infuriate audiences who appreciate the relative qualities of the two media, but one which persists nonetheless. In this present context, the supposed superiority of film is attested through its suitability for addressing children as part of the emotional world of adults. The appeal to human feeling (*ganqing*) is the most appropriate way not just to thread together the young and the old, but also the certainties of past moralities with the challenges of the present.

These threads are strengthened by an institutional culture designed to support the hegemony of the CCP but which also gives longevity to cultural memories, that might otherwise be swept away in the rush to marketisation. Most of the people quoted below are institutionally significant. They have been involved since the 1980s with the Children's Film Studio in Beijing, the China Children's Film Society, and, latterly, the Film Course. The argument here suggests that they are both creative individuals and institutional bearers of *ganqing*, and that accepting them in both roles affords a good sense of how children's media has worked in the past twenty years. Their contributions afford a glimpse of the ways in which people take the past into the present, and indeed illustrate where the past and the present are not so different. In the case of actor and director Yu Lan, strong political links to the Party are crucial to her story, and also to her continuing survival as an iconic figure in children's culture.

Unsurprisingly, her approach to children's film is firmly rooted in her own history of revolutionary cultural work. The institutional context of the work also underpins the gulf between film and television. Children's film-makers seek theatrical release for their work internationally and at home, but only a very few achieve that luxury. The international Christmas releases of 2003— *Peter Pan, The Return of the King, Uptown Girls,* and *Good Boy* are all U.S.-funded family films with a pre-teen audience as a significant source of projected revenue in an extremely competitive market. None of these films (with perhaps the exception of *Good Boy*) are likely to have been (or needed to have been) screened at international children's cinema festivals, the equivalent of the art house circuit for children's film-making worldwide. Most of those will have to opt gratefully for sales direct to video or to cable television.

In China, film is similarly separated from television at the point of production, but most film product for children is most likely to be seen on television—or on VCD—which will be played through a television monitor. The institutional perspectives articulated below are mainly concerned therefore with production values and expectations of ideal theatrical impact, rather than directly confronting the contemporary realities of televisual delivery.

CHILDREN'S FILM

The figure of the child evokes ideas and ideals in a national or cultural imagination, a contention that is true of possibly all cultures and nations to some degree, so this will also affect the ways in which children are addressed in entertainment devised for them by adults. Children's film as a cultural product combines two modes of imagining children. One is to use children in fantasies, which help adults depict the world in which they live, and in which they would like to live. In this world, children are flowers, stars, successors to a perfected future. The other is more market-driven and perhaps of more interest to children themselves; the creation of media product for a specific demographic, or target audience of children. Here children may be all of the above (stars, successors, and hopes) but their images must also reach out to an audience that looks to identify with them in the present. In the children's film culture of the PRC, the emphasis on adult needs has undermined the requirements of a child audience. There are, for instance, characters that show the "bad side of children," but often these "bad children" are symbolic of a bad social reality rather than interestingly wicked characters in themselves. The fat boy in *Sanmao* (1949) is perhaps an exception. He is entertainingly gross and unredeemed, but also represents the corruption of wealth more generally. Other examples after Liberation (1949) are hard to find, however. Film after 1949 is loath to depict any real badness in children, unless it is a failing that can be rectified by the end of the film (as in *Flowers of the Motherland* where both hero and heroine learn to be good children under the guidance of a Korean War veteran). Thus, the redeemed children fulfil the optimism of adult society. When a film is successful it tends to be where the film-maker gives space to childishness: naughtiness, kids' quarrels, and bravado in *Little Soldier Zhangga* are factored in to keep the child audience itself interested in the story. *Little Soldier* thereby ends up as "family entertainment," films which by design or accident please the sensibilities of adults as well as children.

In the history of children's film in China the classics usually fall into that in-between category. Lin Amien, a story-teller and radio presenter turned film director, cites a figure of twenty-three children's films made between 1922 and 1949 which are films for adults as much as children—and yet which are placed in this history of "children's film." Almost all are remembered by name and they hold a place in Chinese cultural history (Lin 2001). Post-Liberation, classic children's titles such as *Chicken Feather Letter* (*Jimao xin*, 1955) and *Little Soldier Zhangga* are remembered as films that people watched together rather than in discrete generational cohorts. These are prototypes of the (revolutionary) family film. Lin argues that, in the current media environment in China, this is the genre, which needs most development if the sector is to survive as a viable player in the market.

Lin argues that the very first children's film in 1923 was an indicator that Chinese cinema had come of age. Film-makers had stopped "playing about" with the medium and had responded to the New Culture Movement (1919) ideals in a serious engagement with social issues and with cinema's place in the drive for change. As a social reformer, Lin refers to the narratives of social action in the 1920s but he is also praising the aesthetic coherence and filmic qualities of the work. Arguably, these new films offered a relevant narrative couched in a stylistically interesting and cinematically derived mode of narration. This contention rests on the assumption that cinema is a modern medium best suited to telling contemporary stories (not necessarily set in the present, but certainly with the mood of the present in mind). *Orphan Saves Grandpa* (*Guer qiu zu ji*) directed in 1923 by Zheng Zhengqiu (1888–1935) and Zhang Shichuan (1889–1953) marks a shift in adult apprehensions of the medium because it can talk about deprivation in emotionally engaging ways for younger people, and thereby provides the starting point for a *history* or *genealogy* of contemporary children's film.[1]

In writing on adult films I have previously touched on the need to look across generations to understand the full range of fantasy structures in play (Donald 2000, 39–43). In looking at the PRC it is also useful to look at alternative genealogies in the Chinese sphere. Before familiarising myself with Mainland and pre-Liberation films, I therefore spent time at the Taibei Film Archive, looking at films *about* children—which were also quite clearly films about Taiwanese identity in the wake of martial law. Films of the early- and mid-1980s were ploughing the furrow of children's hopes and disappointments to make metaphorical attacks on the guttering authoritarianism of Chiang Ching-kuo's Nationalist regime. Film scholars pointed me to the early work of Hou Hsiao-hsien and Edward Yang, but found it hard to recall any films that were notable and *for* children. In Taiwan, it seemed that children occupied a special place in the cinematic imagination, but that their own entertainment was left to television, and especially Japanese animation. Liao Ping-hui and others have argued that the truly transnational impetus in young girls' lives resides in their commitment to *Hello Kitty* websites (Liao Ping-hui 2001; Wu 2002a). Liao and Wu both see Japanese animation as a fashion and lifestyle item rather than anything else, and, even since writing this, their remarks seem prescient. Although *Hello Kitty* merchandise still sells in the Mainland, it is now Korean popular culture that is taking over young hearts, and it will be interesting to see what happens if Korea moves into animation.

Taiwan convinced me that the memories of those who work with children will tell us a great deal about their intentions in a cultural but also historical context, and about the local conventions with which children negotiate their uses of media. Taiwan has a small but talented film industry with only minimal public support. Co-productions with Hong Kong and the Mainland are increasingly common. The Film Archives are themselves housed in a small block in central Taibei, and in 1998 were concerned about maintaining their film stock and even in keeping the storage conditions to standard for their current holdings. Film does not hold the educational focus that it enjoys in Mainland China, and the difference in approach to children's film-making is striking. Whereas in both societies children watch more television than they do film, there is a continuing belief in film as a medium for cultural and social education in China; hence the institutional investment in film. This is in part due to the influence of older people in the business, mainly actors, directors, and radio producers, who retain the somewhat nostalgic motivation expressed in Yu Lan's comment that "You see, if children are not guided correctly they can easily become corrupted."

THE CHILDREN'S STUDIO

The Beijing (later the China) Children's Film Studio (CCFS) was established with the approval and endorsement of the Ministry of Culture in March 1981, and opened on 1 June, in direct response to a call a few months earlier by the Central Committee "for all society to pay heed to the healthy growth of the young" ("*quan dang quan shehui dou yao guanxin shaonian ertong de jiankang chengchang*").[2] The Studio's original objectives were to make good films for children and to thereby promote children's socialist education. The Studio is very much a creature of its time, a last-ditch attempt by the government to promote a cultural field that prioritises the appropriate socialisation of successors to the Communist Party and its erstwhile ideals. Its ideological baseline, and therefore its product, suffered—and to a large extent still suffers—from the contradictions inherent in Deng Xiao-ping's reform plan. The early 1980s posed difficult options for cultural life, given the intimate relation between politics and creativity over the previous thirty years. On the one hand, all endeavours must be oriented towards money-making, but on the other, there must be no radical shift in the political culture, nor a drift towards "spiritual pollution." Yet, there must also be a move away from Maoist interpretations of Marxist-Leninism, and therefore a de-politicisation of cultural activity; "The Dengist project of the reformers and their successors had a twofold task: to bury the revolutionary political culture and instil a political culture attuned to a market oriented economy" (Benewick and Donald 2003, 79). The four basic principles of thought in Deng's socialist culture forestalled a legitimate reworking of appropriate values for the new era. Perry Link and Kate Zhou have summarised the guidelines as "curious . . . in one sense far removed from daily life, but in another sense deadly serious" (2002, 99). The post-revolutionary, but not post-CCP state, values which the state-sponsored studios and their senior leaders still support hold another thread into the present and future through these overwhelming dictums of policy and approach.

In principle then, Yu Lan's role in the 1980s as director of the new Studio was to implement a spiritually "unpolluted" system of values to children, based on the four principles of adherence to the socialist road, the dictatorship of the proletariat, the leadership of the Communist Party, and Marxist-Leninist-Maoist thought. However, Mao himself and the ways in which his regime had implemented those principles, particularly over the previous fifteen years, was to be sidelined. In principle, her task was impossible. Children's film was already being "polluted" by the influx of pirate Disney, by Japanese animation on television, and by what Watson has named the "McDonaldisation" of everyday cultural pleasure (Watson 1997). In practice, the Studio has been served and staffed by committed film-makers and performers, many of whom who have had previous experience in the entertainment industries, and some of whom have gone on to international renown. The need to save children from corrupting influences has necessitated the construction of an internal system of values that are affective, rather than politically pragmatic but empty "basic principles." As will be explored in the analysis of *Heavenly Kite* (below), one strategy has been to compound the recuperated idealism of the very old with the naive optimism of the young, and thereby to bypass the greed of the adult world.

In discussing her work with the Children's Film Studio, Yu Lan seems to talk about a way of being that she wishes to purify and then transmit to new generations. These discussions took place over four years and made it clear that the educative imperative of children's film in China is not just about the young. Yu Lan is a woman in her early eighties, with a track record across almost seventy years of pre-Liberation and revolutionary culture. She has been an actress for most of her life, with a painful break point in the Cultural Revolution and a return to prominence behind the camera as producer and director of films for children. The first interview was a piece of good luck. Due to a family connection, my research associate effected an introduction. The meeting had not been planned as part of the trip and was at first fraught with nervousness. How, after all, do you speak with someone whose face had for forty years epitomised the courage and strength of revolutionary energy and intransigence? How do you ask naïve questions about media and socialisation of a woman who has been everywhere in recent Chinese history, (the first photograph of her with her equally famous actor [and director of the Beijing Film Studio] husband Tian Fang was taken in 1940 at Yenan)? Not only had she been everywhere, she had also performed the epitome of revolutionary fantasy in the lives of many millions of other Chinese. The moment in a more recent conversation (2002) when she seemed most herself was in her response to the question, "How does being an actress help you in your current work?" She looked momentarily surprised and then said simply, "Actors need to understand other people, so we know what children feel." Whatever her recent history as a manager, director, and motivational leader of the children's film movement, she was first and memorably an actress.

My introduction to Chinese film had been, like so many others of my generation, through the passionate and brilliant commentaries of Tony Rayns and Derek Elley at the London Film Festivals and retrospectives in the late 1980s and early 1990s. Film stars were not visible to me in these film experiences except where a particular performance stood out, or was pointed out in critical assessment. I had seen Yu Lan's seminal performance in *Revolutionary Family* (*Geming jiating* 1960) whilst sitting in the library stacks in the Oriental Institute Heidelberg, but I had no real idea of what or whom I was watching, and why she mattered. Even when a fellow researcher, a fifty-something Chinese academic paused in his tracks and stood behind me, watching the film on the small monitor in a cramped space for over an hour,

I did not quite "get it." Yu Lan's significance as an actress is that she played many revolutionary roles, especially mothers, but reemerged after the Cultural Revolution as the "mother" of children's film. She represents therefore a peculiar continuity of moral and political will that leapfrogs the end of the Maoist era, into the Reform period. In her time Yu Lan played brave nurses, romantic but committed fighters, and the mother in *Soldiers in White* (*Baiyi zhanshi* 1948), *Red Flag at Cui Gang* (*Cui gang hongqi* 1950), *Dragon Bear Ditch* (*Longxu gou* 1953), and *Revolutionary Family* (*Geming jiating*). She was the imprisoned heroine in *Living in the Flames of War* (*Liehuo zhong yongshengi* 1965). She was the woman whose baby was trampled to death by the crowd at the chaotic finale to *Lin Family Shop* (*Linjia puzi* 1959). Her credentials as a maternal figure in revolutionary cultural memory are impeccable. Her life story, especially the romance and marriage with Tian Fang but—especially—the unusual happy ending with a new career, has been immortalised in hagiographic publications.

Despite her transformation into the mother of children's film, it is not hard to recognise the actress in her. She is poised, elegant, aware always of her public significance, and also prone to giggles. When my colleague offered her a fur hat made from kangaroo and rabbit skin as a gift (a real Australian hybrid), she immediately put it on and kept it on for the duration of the interview. As that first conversation progressed, and she touched an invisible scar on her cheek whilst talking about her disappearance from the screen in the 1970s, it also became clear that Yu Lan bore her history as physically as she performed her glamour.

Her past fame and her current high status in the cultural establishment make her part of the old guard. She presents, however, a more sympathetic picture of the old and the established in Chinese public life than do the political leaders who are her contemporaries, and with whom most readers will be more familiar. She makes it possible to perceive the difficulty of moving from a revolutionary and nationalist media environment to one that needs to take into account the creative demands and cosmopolitan awareness of its children. Her growth as an actress and latterly as a director and producer and public representative of children's film were rooted in a childhood in pre-Liberation China, an acting career that represented the new ideas of new China, and which spanned a civil war, liberation, revolutionary social change, and a cultural revolution which nearly destroyed her. Now in an equally extraordinary reform period, she has found herself representing old values to new generations.

Yu Lan and others of her generation stand out now as retaining a deep, younger people might think perverse, commitment to something like revolutionary purity (*kongbai*) but which might be better understood as a faith in the child as a marker of Chinese stability. In the course of a discussion about China's modern history she volunteered the following account of her life as inseparable from those events, and on an inevitable continuum with the work of educating and entertaining children. She is convinced of the threads running between past and present, and of the continuing impact of moral decisions made long ago, on the way in which she understands herself now. Her story is unforgiving of other perspectives on history, "we" refers to those who see history the way she sees it, "they" are later generations who do not see the urgency of a correct decision, whilst those who presumably made the wrong decision (those for example who stayed and worked as film-makers in Shanghai) are not mentioned at all.

But what kind of person am I? I couldn't do that [work with the Japanese or be a housewife]. I had to leave. I went to join other anti-Japanese people. You see, my experience . . . I was an actress [Yu Lan used the term *huaji* which implies that actresses seduce men and were held by others in low esteem]. But actresses also want love and also want a real career. But there was nothing for us. I wanted to join the anti-Japanese struggle. I wanted to seek a goal of survival and of really living. Where could I go? That was a big question for me.

In 1937 the Japanese occupied Beijing and the following year I left home by myself. The Japanese had earlier occupied my home, Manchuria. So I came to study in Beijing. But they came to Beijing too. I had to leave. The first time, I was only ten years old. I didn't really understand what had happened. But the second time I was sixteen. In the intervening period we had witnessed many insulting agreements [between China and foreign powers]. We hated our government [National Party—Guomindang] at that time. But we also hoped that they would save us, even though they had run away. We hoped that they wouldn't let us live under the Japanese. But they didn't come. So how would you choose your road? There were so many, so many people like us. They were not like contemporary people who say "Wow! Why did you have to suffer so much?" When the Communists came you joined the revolution, that's just what you did.

Anyway, they say, it doesn't matter who joined first and who joined last. But of course there is a difference! Have you contributed to the nation (*minzu*)? People would have asked that. We respect you, they say, because you joined, . . . and it was because I had read so much and had a certain cultural understanding (*wenhua shuyang*) that I didn't want to live and work under the Japanese. (interview 1999)

So, in responding to a query about political stability and children's media, Yu Lan delves right back to her defining moment as a person—"Who am I?" Her answer is that she is an actress, but also a person with a profound knowledge of the culture in which she has been so prominent, and which has a definite revolutionary edge. In the historical circumstance in which she lived she found that all of these parts of herself could only be fulfilled if she contributed to the "good" of a Chinese nation. Her first political goal was contributing to the anti-Japanese struggle in the 1930s. It led her to similar-minded young people, to the Communist Party, and eventually to a career in revolutionary drama. On her return to political favour after the Cultural Revolution she was invited to run the Children's Film Studio.

In her interviews Yu Lan scarcely alluded to her suffering in the late 1960s, although she (and her son, Tian Zhuangzhuang) concurred that much of the boy's memories presented in Tian's (banned) 1993 film *The Blue Kite* were based on experience. Those memories include a mother sent away to remote regions to labour, and a prevailing feeling of dislocation between family love and political demands. The film also suggests a deep and romantic attachment between the boy's parents, fortunately one that was not cut short in life as it was in the film. But, in the last sequence of the film, her son picks up a brick and hits a teenager who has bullied his mother. He is beaten up and left bleeding on the ground. Perhaps due to memories like these, even if not exactly as portrayed in the film, Yu Lan retains a worry about the production of "bad" children, and the responsibility of cultural workers to mitigate the perils of modern life. That is the work, which she has pursued through the Studio.

The Studio has also supported the careers of young film-makers entering the industry. Zhang Jianya and Zhang Yimou worked there briefly on *Red Elephant (Hong Xiang)* alongside Tian Zhuanzhuang in 1982 (an account is offered in Ni and Berry 2003). Peng Xiaolian also began her career there (*Me and My Classmates*). The Studio has also always had its own production team as well as a good source of volunteer talent from other studios and from the Beijing Film Academy. This makes it both prolific and economic. In the first year it produced two films: *Four Little Playmates (sige xiao huoban)* and *Su Xiaosan*. In the second year it produced four, one of which, *Red Elephant*, was its first foray into minority themes. From 1983 to 1985 the Studio produced three films a year and from then until 2001, an average of five films a year.[3] Every two years the ten or so films compete for the Golden Calf award. Minority and rural themes crop up regularly, as well as an increasing concern with family breakdown, and related modern pressures on children's lives. (The Shanghai Film Studio continued to be the main domestic source of children's animation in this period, but only recently has it considered challenging the CCFS in live action.) Some of the CCFS's films work very well, treading a line between moral purity and the real challenges facing real children. *Don't Cry Mummy (Bieku mama)* is an example of a clever account of a child's work as a carer in a broken family, choosing between a father who offers a materially comfortable life, and an impoverished mother whose mental illness requires that her son give her constant attention. As I have argued elsewhere (2000), this film is also artistically adept, and carries forward the tradition of the family-oriented drama that Lin Amien identifies from the 1920s.

Others are less successful artistically sometimes because the scope and ambition of the story is not matched by access to software editing and special effects packages that match the expectations of a modern audience. *The Atmospheric Layer Vanishes* (*Da qiceng xiaoshi* 1990) suffers from this, although in conception it is very interesting, The film was directed by a Beijing Film Academy graduate (Feng Xiaoning, graduated 1982) and stars the wonderful actress, Lü Liping.[4] The plot is, briefly, that a train carrying deadly gases is derailed and the poison seeps out, threatening to destroy life on earth. A small boy finds he can speak to animals and goes with a cat, a dog, a bank robber, and a criminal truck driver to save the world. The film ends with television broadcasts debating the end of the ozone layer and the imminent collapse of the world's atmosphere. Feng Xiaoning, a younger man than the Studio's elders and with a less recognisably "pure" (*kongbai*) version of how people should "feel," gives his reasons for making the film:

> In 1988, the UN published a list of the worst polluted cities in the world. Shenyang was second on the list, Xian was eighth and Beijing ninth, so China topped the world in air pollution. Yet our heavy industries were not doing anything about the way they work in line with other parts of the world. . . . A film can't solve the problem of air pollution, nor can it offer an adequate analysis of the problem . . . but it can show children what's what (*women zhi shi rang haizimen zhidao*). The film serves only as an alarm.[5]

The film is underedited and cannot deliver on either the action sequences or special effects. It is an example of a good idea with not enough money or technical expertise to back it up, and it exemplifies the problems that the Studio has more recently experienced with digital animation. If the Studio tries to challenge Pixar and Hollywood in what they do best, the failure is depressing (Donald 2002). Nevertheless, there is something in the intentions of the film that is heartening. Feng wants to let the children know what is what (*rang haizimen zhidao*). The educative imperative is here nuanced by an admission that adults do not have the answers, or if they do, they are not acting on them in the best interests of either children or animals. This approach to cultural education is a long way from the four basics of Deng and is an updated example of what I am calling *ganqing*—a tensile thread of human feeling between children and their cinematic collocutors at the Studio, which is contemporary as well as nostalgic.

CHILDREN'S FILM SCHOLARSHIP

In December 1984 another institutional support was added to children's film and the drive against spiritual pollution. The Children's Film Society was established to support the work of the studio through intellectual and academic endeavours, and through bringing the importance of children's film to the attention of researchers and educators. Its dictum is that "one good film can influence the whole life of a child" (*yibu haode zuopin changhui yingxiang haizi de yisheng*). Its membership was drawn from the great and the good in all spheres of children's media and arts and its existence is a statement of the state's concern with children's media. The society also makes bridges between the Studio and other studios making children's films. It selects and publishes the Golden Calf awards, and generally coordinates the public face of Chinese film production for the young. Its work is one of validation, through the construction of a historical genealogy of value in the sector.

Children's film history has been divided into six periods (Zheng 1999), thus differentiating it from the generational divides suggested for adult cinema (although the chronologies are much the same). The first period, exemplified by the work of Zheng Zhengqiu, is concentrated in the 1920s and 1930s. Most characters are urban waifs, and the tone is of social comment. The first children's film in Chinese cinema was *Wantong* (*Naughty Child* 1922). *Orphan Saves His Grandpa* (1923) is the earliest film still extant, however, and tends to be cited as a major title, as is Cai Chusheng's *Lost Lamb* (*Mitu de gaoyang*) (1935). Both films are concerned with the suffering of children in war, and treat of the feelings between adults and the young as the world collapses around them. These films are remembered for their political content, the plight of street urchins in Shanghai, but also for their lightness of touch. A clearly child-oriented film with extraordinary merit, both in terms of its grotesque realisation and of its social credentials, is *Sanmao's Travels* (*Sanmao liulang ji* 1949), based on Zhang Louping's cartoon strip of the little three-haired boy urchin in Shanghai. This film is semi-cartoon in mode, as the pantomimic characterisation relieves the tragedy of its subject matter. The main character, a bulbous-nosed, three-haired waif should be sad (a lost lamb) but is in fact resourceful and very naughty (the original *wantong*). A later version of *Sanmao* from the Shanghai Studio *Sanmao congjun ji* (*Sanmao Joins the Army*) tried to recapture the humour and cartoon anarchy of the original, but was too concerned with making specific political connections between the child and his environment to truly succeed. One young director cited this latter film as an example of the failure of Chinese children's film since 1949 "to use Sanmao as an educational figure has already lost the meaning of a children's film."[6] The same interviewee argued that children's films have been treated as a "type of dish, a meal, an achievement," but not, he suggests, looking much beyond the direct educational needs of the audience. The "seventeen years" period from 1949–1966 was mainly focused on the revolution, on war, and on building a new life in a social democracy. The famous *Little Soldier Zhangga* and the shepherd boy from *Chicken Feather Letter* are from this period and these films do manage to convey entertainment as well as social education. Both protagonists are also children who are poor and who are fighting for a rosy and explicitly politicised future. In the 1966–1974 Cultural Revolution period there was only one live action film specifically made for children, *Sparkling Red Star* (1974). The film is set between 1931–1938, and treats of successes in liberating villages, and the subsequent reprisals, horrors, and eventual triumph of the peasants under the leadership of Dongzi's father, a commander in the Jiangnan Division of the Red Army. Dongzi, the young hero in *Sparkling Red Star*, sees his mother burned alive and is involved in fierce fighting. He is spurred on by the gift of a red star given to him by his father, who, for most of the film, is absent fighting. Dongzi, like his earlier counterparts in children's film, is striving for the revolution, but with no humour and little childish wit. It is as though the relaxed address to children as partners in a project to build the nation, which is the overall impression of films made in the 1950s and 1960s, gives way to a more desperate attempt to retrieve childhood in a paranoid expression of the chaos of political culture at the time. The film is shot in full Chinese technicolour, reminiscent of the dramatic personality of Douglas Sirk melodrama or the visual excess of a Hollywood musical on old Technicolor. The film is far less concerned with the childish character of its subjects than were the solid but more gentle adventure stories of the "seventeen years." The brightness and lack of gradation in the colour tone matched the undifferentiated address to children and adults as patriots at the tail end of a period of political excess.

In 1976 film-making resumed; in 1978 film training was reorganised at the Beijing Film Academy (2003), and cultural workers returned to the studios. In 1979 (the international year of the child) seasoned professionals produced films for children that were of obvious artistic merit and which "opened up" ways of seeing and thinking for a new era. Wang Junzhao's *Miaomiao* (1979) and Xie Jin's war film for adults and children, *The Cradle* (*A Yaolan* 1979), are the most significant in this emerging category of post–Cultural Revolution cinema, and represent a return to national expressivity and cultural (rather than absolute political) aesthetics (Zheng 1999, 96). Xie Jin's work in *The Cradle* is particularly skillful in this respect. The film follows a group of children whose parents are fighting for the Communist forces, and who have been isolated by a series of Japanese attacks on their camp. Three soldiers (two women and a man) are sent to bring them to safety and reunite them with their parents. The story is partly an adventure and partly a drama surrounding the mixed feelings of soldiers who are given the job of nursemaid when they would prefer to be at the front. As they discover parental feelings they also realise that the war is meaningless without young people to succeed to a new China, and they grow as people as well as heroes in the process. The film thereby deconstructs the *Shanshan* image of indestructible and infallible revolutionaries. The people in this film are valued for their warmth, for an ability to compromise ideals for the survival of human feeling (again, *ganqing*), and for their prioritisation of family life. Seen from the perspective of post-feminism it does seem to get women out of uniform and back to the nursery, but, taken in the spirit of 1979, the film is an extraordinary intervention. The film refutes the generational splits that were encouraged in the late 1960s and advocates self-inquiry and personal growth. In this film children are brave and they all receive military medals at the conclusion of their journey. But, above all, they are happy to see their parents and their parents clearly need to see them. Human happiness is a virtue not a sign of weakness.

In *The Cradle* Xie Jin explores the post–Cultural Revolution era through the vehicle of a seemingly classic "family war film"—the genre that includes *Little Soldier*, *Chicken Feather Letter*, and *Living in the Flames of War*. The film was even made at the August 1st Studio, which is attached to the PLA (Peoples' Liberation Army). There are, however, significant differences. The enemy is hardly seen except through scenes of devastation, and in one sequence when they shoot (and miss) at a toddler who wanders into their sight. In the ensuing battle another child is killed, but we do not see the killer. In the set-piece sequences where two leading characters survey a beautiful landscape and dream of a (Red) Chinese China (*zhonghua minzu guo*), they do so as humans who are, subtly but unmistakably, falling in love. There is also a short sequence where the children find a large roadside Buddha. They recognise it and clamber on it, and one child pretends to pray. The children laugh at his antics and the sequence is not especially respectful of the religion. Nor, however, is it condemnatory. Whereas ten years before the children would have been expected to destroy the statue as a dangerous relic of the "four olds," now they play. Nevertheless, *The Cradle* is a serious film. It addresses children as very competent viewers, asking them to understand adults as flawed whilst also accepting that they are essentially good, and that the thread between parents and children is fundamental to happiness. This may seem a truism in the wonderful world of Disney, but it was a statement of some emotional impact in the wake of the Cultural Revolution.

INFLUENCES

Sixteen years earlier, *Little Wooden Head* (*Xiaolingdang* 1963) was directed by an actor-director, Xie Tian (1914–2003). *Little Wooden Head* seemed to emerge from an older imagination from that which produced the seriousness in children's films directly after the Cultural Revolution. Xie Tian had a long career as an actor from the 1930s through 1960s. He was still taking occasional roles in 1998 but his acting star appeared to have waned considerably with the release of *Lin Family Shop* in 1959 (*linjia puzi*), a family melodrama with more than a hint of bourgeois sentiment. However, he continued as a children's director and made several classic films, including *Flower Garden* (*Huar er duoduo*) and *Xiaolingdang*.

Xie Tian claims that his earliest introduction to films was the work of Charlie Chaplin, the socially conscious clown of early American silent cinema. He remembers that as a young boy he would dress up and perform Charlie Chaplin acts for his family and for other children in his courtyard:

> As my father worked in a railway station, I grew up in a working class family. My father was Cantonese but I grew up in Tianjin. I loved films from the beginning. You know why? Because my parents were big Charlie Chaplin fans. My mother adored him. I loved to watch him too. If my Mother thought he was good, I did too. Sometimes she would take me to see his films everyday. At that time film meant Chaplin and Chaplin meant film. People used to say they were going to see Chaplin (*kan* Chaplin) even when it wasn't a Chaplin film. I was hugely influenced by his work. That was why I made comedy films. The other big influence was Disney. I don't really want to go anywhere, but I do want to go to Disneyland, not Los Angeles, not New York, not Hollywood. But oh that Chaplin! He can act anything, but at the same time no one could understand him. He is like a cartoon. His films are not divided by national boundaries. They have real themes and content. You see, because he came from a poor background he suffered a lot when he was young. I have read his autobiography over and over. [Interviewer: Are there any Chinese film-makers you admire?] Ha! No one you could remember! [*more Chaplin reminiscences*] When I was a child I played *za baozi* [throwing pictures/card flicking]. You'd flick the picture-cards from cigarette packets. I always lost, I lost lots of pictures. When I got home I would ask for more and my father said "how many cigarettes do I have to smoke to keep you playing?" Anyway my Father thought of a way to win some pictures. He asked me to perform Chaplin skits to attract an audience. I used to do that for my parents and my Mother loved my performances. The more she saw me perform the happier she was. My father suggested that my sister make a stage for me in the courtyard, every child had to pay two pictures for entry . . . this is the beginning of my career.[7]

The memories of Xie Tian are very like those of Yu Lan: both tend towards a moment of decision, the tipping point that pushed the speaker's life one direction or another; Yu Lan was an actress but needed to make sense of that role in a war-torn society. Xie Tian counts his defining moment as the time he became an actor. He is decisive on that point. Unlike Yu Lan, whose influences were historical and somewhat monumental, Xie was influenced by his mother and by Charlie Chaplin (and managed by his father and sister). Xie Tian's memories are therefore both domestic and international and far less overtly tied to a national (*minzu*) consciousness than are those of Yu Lan. Xie Tian's memories of Chaplin are for him the epitome of his cinematic experience, and his ongoing enthusiasm underlines the affect of cinema for

a young audience, and the potential of that affect to define lives. He also remembers the cinema entwined with his attachment to his mother and his
family, again part of an overriding drive to retain family connections within
mediated versions of everyday and extraordinary life. Yu Lan regrets her absent father and her lost mother in the same breath as she remembers seeing
left-wing films and deciding to be active in the anti-Japanese movement. Xie
Tian later remembered his professional debut and his travels in China (which
admittedly started a few months before the Sino-Japanese War), but at no
point does he make a connection between his work and politics—it is all
about family connections:

> Then at school I met Shen Fu. He worked as a newspaper editor eventually.
> . . . He loved Chaplin, and so did I. We both loved films. Later Luo Mingyou in-
> vited him to work in Mingxing [Studios] in Shanghai. I was so happy. In 1935 I
> left Beijing for Shanghai. My father saw me off. I was only twenty-one and I was
> brave. I had never left home before, and I couldn't believe that this would be
> the last time I saw my father. I went to Shanghai and worked with a theatre com-
> pany. Then I went to Lianhua [Studios] to see Shen Fu [Xie Tian seems to have
> mixed up which studios his friend actually worked for at this point—or maybe
> he had moved]. He told me "well I would like to have you but we have no
> money at the moment." The film business is in a bad way and we havn't been
> able to pay salaries for three months. Well I was really lost and I went back to
> working in theatre. Anyway, you know Hu Dian the actress, the queen of Chi-
> nese cinema I should say. Well, her father and my father used to work together
> in the railway company and . . . she introduced me to Hong Sheng.

Xie Tian continues explaining how a family connection got him his first
break in film, how he chose not to go to Hong Kong along with the director
of that film, Li Pingqian, because his mother was in Beijing, and eventually the
subject of left-wing filmmakers comes up. He describes how he admired such
work—and indeed joined the Shanghai Amateur Film Theatre Workers' Association for a spell. Eventually, however, he went to Chongqing—following
the Guomindang (Nationalist) anti-Japanese struggle—where he made films
with Shen Fu and earned a reputation as a comedian. Despite the Nationalist
element, in Yu Lan's historiography this counts as a good move as it takes him
away from the Japanese influences in the Shanghai cinema. He started di-
recting in 1957, and suffered three criticisms in the Cultural Revolution from
Jiang Qing, Mao's then-wife and former actress. He remembers the attacks as
personally vindictive; he thought she resented him for having made too many
films when she herself was a rather insignificant bit player in the Association.
This part of the story is a tacked-on response to a direct question. He does not
dwell on that time, nor on the effect on his wife who was permanently trau-
matised by the cruelties. He does ask us, however, to go in and say hello to
her before we leave, so she doesn't get scared and jealous again. He does not

elucidate what exactly might be scaring her, but indicates that she has not been well since the Cultural Revolution. Yu Lan carries her scar in her face, but Xie Tian lived loyally alongside a terrified woman for over thirty years.

Xie Tian's recount of his history is not a random set of recollections. He is a much-interviewed person and he has been the subject of at least one documentary. Indeed, the day we met him—an interview that lasted from 8:30 AM until 3:00 PM—Xie Tian proudly told us that a journalist had recently visited him and asked for ten minutes yet became caught in his stories for three hours. Xie Tian's narrative is an interesting foil to Yu Lan's memories. Yu Lan is always an actress but her art is pursued through politically inspired decisions. Xie Tian is a comedian who happens to have lived through a politically volatile period of history. His self-characterisation rests on his humour, "I can't act in a tragedy as people always laugh at me. Look at Chaplin, if he tried for tragedy, people would laugh." He does not discuss political difficulties that he experienced with *Lin Family Shop* (1959) because of his work in Chongqing during the war, nor does he openly regret having chosen to stay in China near his mother rather than leave for Hong Kong or Taiwan. In that sense his self-characterisation is only partly accurate. He is Chaplinesque because there is a great deal of tragedy in his clowning and because he classifies his life through his childhood.[8] Indeed, he sums up his decisions and achievements as a series of responses to his childhood drive to please his beloved mother and to be as funny as Charlie Chaplin.

The coda to Xie Tian's story is the 1980s Children's Film Studio reprise of his 1963 film, *Little Wooden Head*. Xie Tian was a founding member of the Children's Film Society, in the records of which he is listed as a "very famous film artiste" (*dianying yishu jia*), which refers mainly to his acting career but also perhaps to his work as a director. In 1986 he made *Little Wooden Head* (the sequel). The film is first and foremost a visually literate children's film that still makes children laugh out loud (this assertion is based on an imperfect research method—I have shown it to children who do, and children who do not, speak Chinese. They all laugh). The central character is still the little Xiaolingdang, a pre-schooler puppet with wingnut ears, a few black hairs, and a prominent nose, who falls somewhere between Sanmao, the three-haired scamp, and Pinocchio, the Italian wooden marionette with a penchant for trouble.

The second point of interest is that, given Xie Tian's memories, it is hard not to associate *Xiaolingdang* also with Chaplin, the man who seems like a cartoon because of his puppet-like mode of being, both affective and strangely inhuman, that distances him from the people in his own stories but endears him to the crowd. The *Little Wooden Head* movie of 1986, and its original in 1963, fulfills one of the strongest calls from the child interviewees in our discussions on an ideal children's film:[9] it is local, it blends cartoon fantasy with real life familiarity and empathy, and it has a reach beyond language. Also, and this applies to the 1986 film, it is acutely aware of television and of a general modernisation of children's ecologies of pleasure. Much of the plot's impetus concerns treats for Children's Day; these include a trip to a television studio, a visit to a science exhibit, and a chance to work on banks of PCs (in 1986 these constituted something close to science fiction in the lives of most primary school children in most parts of the world). It also contains puppet shows that draw on the animated films of the Shanghai studios, and therefore also on the puppet animations and storytelling slots screened daily on CCTV 7 and BTV. The film serves its amusements up in televisual-size bites, no individual section is longer than the average twenty minutes of a Shanghai-made animation short or of a television show segment.

As the film opens, it is Children's Day and a small group of Grade Ones have just been treated to a screening of the original *Xiaolingdang*. They desperately want to find him to play. First they try searching out the original child actors, but they have grown up and become a policeman and a cellist, and no longer have the imagination to find the secrets of a wooden doll. Then the leader of the children, Xiao Pang, goes home and drifts into a dream in which his robot toy, a red, plastic, Made in China symbol of economic reform, comes to life and helps him track down the puppet with the help of the puppet maker's wife (played by Yu Lan's contemporary Tian Hua). Most of the story revolves around Xiaolingdang making friends with adults who remember him from their childhoods, and his exploits in a new modernised Beijing. Through Xiaolingdang's eyes we see how tall the buildings have grown, how amazing are the new amusement parks at Chaoyang, and how extraordinary the fashion shows, television quizzes, and electronic equipment with which the children themselves are utterly familiar.

What might have been an eccentric trip down memory lane for parents is very much, however, a film for children. The gags are Chaplinesque. They work because of the character of the puppet. He is a showman, used to being entertaining and needing to be funny and loved. His need gives him the potential for tragedy, headed off by a joke when it threatens to overwhelm. When he discovers an electric piano in a television studio, he is desperate to show off, and a producer who recognises him from the past allows him to use it. His happiness at his ability to play is matched by the child audience's amused sympathy as they realise that the puppet does not understand that the piano's electronic memory is doing at least as much work as he (that said, the children who watched it with me in 2002 assumed that it must be a super smart Yamaha digital piano, an anachronism that simply compounded their pity for the puppet). At a fashion show he gets up on stage and shows off his new clothes, given to him by shop assistants who remember him from their childhoods. Here he excels, as he is indeed the clown who is funniest when most out of place. Eventually, the robot—who has been constantly teasing him about his lack of schooling for someone who is, after all, over twenty years old—challenges him to a quiz on television. Rows of solemn Young Pioneers sit waiting for the correct answers, as the sweet BTV hostess-teacher figure poses questions related to modern education. Xiaolingdang tries bravely to joke his way through but the crunch comes when she asks the toys to show what they can do in a foreign language. The puppet proudly recites his alphabet. The robot reels off a series of pat phrases in five languages, and Xiaolingdang makes for the door. At that moment the film takes its little clown very seriously. The children find him slumped against the corridor wall, miserable and humiliated by his educational shortcomings. It takes several more adventures before he regains his confidence and his sense of self worth in this world of new competencies and clever children.

Xiaolingdang 2 is a small film, dependent on television for its structure, although also making the point perhaps that television has learnt a great deal from the film's earlier formation and from Xie Tian's *Huar er duorduor*, also constructed around entertaining variety sequences. *Xiaolingdang 2* is also significant as a film, making as it does a conscious attempt to bridge the gap between generations. In a way, this is all that the Children's Film Studio and its supporters have ever sought to achieve.

GANQING

Picture a yellow kite fluttering in an empty sky, the sound of a child singing below, out of frame. Imagine this kite decorated with a smiling face, flying strongly in the breeze on a lovely spring Beijing day, the red walls of a Ming tower cradling the kite flyers from any hint of wind chill. This yellow flutter is emblematic of a perfect childhood, and this is the opening sequence of *Heavenly Letter* (*Tiantang huixin* 1992), a Beijing Film Studio production, and a film that comes highly recommended by many of the Children's Film Society, Love Children Society, and Children's Studio's senior, older staff. The film's motif echoes the 1950s tale *Kite* (*Fengzheng* 1956, co-production China/France) of a rogue "Monkey" kite that flies to France to recruit little international friends for children in Beijing. It also prefigures the 1993 *Blue Kite*, which uses very similar sequences to top and tail a much more sombre version of childhood in the PRC.

As the camera pans down, leaving the kite string thinly visible in shot, we discover a small boy and an old man, both palpably delighted with the kite, their play, and one another. Cycling home the tiny boy takes the handlebars and gives his tired grandfather a ride by the canal, as passersby cheer him on: "*jia you*"! Poignantly, this idyllic relationship is built on absence. The boy's mother is away overseas earning money, and the grandfather has been bringing the boy up for two years. When the mother returns she disrupts their routine of happy companionship and mutual reliance. It is, after all, hard to establish a regime of utilitarian modernity where the existing status quo is based on pleasure and play. The boy and grandfather communicate in ways that are too irrational for her "foreign" sensibility. They play constantly, and they have unspoken friendships with people who they meet habitually on their way about the city. Occasionally they "work" together, the boy helping on the mail route (his grandfather is a postman). The title of the film refers to their use of kites to "fly" letters to those who have died and "gone away," somewhere like Heaven. Thus the older man teaches the boy that a profession is built on responsibility and human feeling for one's clients. In the final scene, the boy, a small friend, and another old man use the same route to "mail" a birthday card to the recently deceased grandfather.

The string of the kite in Tian Zhuangzhuang's film symbolises the constraints of life in China.[10] In *Heavenly Letter* the string is closer to a metaphor for *ganqing* (human feeling) that ties together the old and the young, the past and the present, in a secure, virtuous, and humane relationship. The danger of modernisation, as exemplified in the character of the mother, is that she has lost that subtle tension between generations and family members. She has forgotten that feeling is mutual, imaginative, and symbolic. When she clears away the boy's pet guinea pigs into the kitchen and the cage falls out the window, both are killed. The film does not hold back on the blood or the stumbling suffering of the little creatures, nor on the boy's huge anger and sorrow at their deaths. The depth of a small boy's feeling for small rodents is no less than the developed competency that is the *ganqing* between adults and children, between adults and adults, and which—finally—helps people answer Yu Lan's questions. Who am I? Where should I have gone?

There is also a somewhat melodramatic affect underlying this film, and this is not uncommon to other children's film. This affective component of narrative is based on a principle of harmony within hierarchy; that, in a functioning society, the very young and the senior members of the population are mutually defined. They address one another with human feeling, recognising one another as figures in a shared culture. In cinematic terms this human feeling is melodramatically achieved through nostalgia, historical events, and detailed memories of small incidents that remind the audience of their own lives and their own historical context. In giving an account of a *children's* film studio I have therefore also emphasised the importance of older people and their recall of their own trajectories of socialisation.

Public engagement, "publicness," also pertains to thinking about cinema and its assumed audiences. Publicness is a term that seeks to escape the benevolent proscriptions of liberal democracy and "civil society;" it refers rather to communicative success between medium and audience, between audience and collective, and—occasionally—between collective and national communicative space. In children's media, publicness is found primarily in moments of recognition, passages of memory, and symptoms of nostalgia in Chinese culture for, and of, the young. It is also, if we take account that thin but tensile kite string of human feeling, about the old and the ageing, and the memories that they choose to recall. It is about what priorities are passed on, what threads of memory and feeling produce as a set of shared competencies between old and young, past and present.

In a conversation with the director of *The Blue Kite* I noted that some of his apparent opposition to the studio run by his mother (Yu Lan) was somewhat contradictory. This was not, I think, a deliberate contradiction, but one rather that arises between generations who misrecognise the patterns that are passed to them by their elders, or taken up differently by their children. In this conversation, Tian Zhuangzhuang argued that *The Blue Kite* was not a film about childhood but rather a film that opportunistically structures itself around the event-based memories of a child. As he explained what he meant by this, an argument about plot structure and the production of meaning through the establishment of narrative form, he also talked about the spaces that young people require through which to find themselves and their direction in life.

> Because history is in a distant past, we don't remember things too well . . . a child remembers days, events; this was a happy day, this was a day of suffering, this day was important, this was the day he got that present . . . this character [in *The Blue Kite*] is created to structure the film. He does not represent the value and meaning of all children. He is important though for two things: his function in the structure [of the film's memory], and the way in which he shows a child's growth—how does he grow up to be the kind of person that he is? Lots of what happens to him is hardly noticed, it is unconscious [and therefore not visible in the structure of the film]. In the end, the one conscious thing that he does is rebel. He can't tolerate suppression any longer. So from all the different barely conscious events in his life he finally wakes up (*wudao*) as a rebel. That is what I mean when I say that the boy is a major string (*yi tiaoxian*) in the structure of the film. It is also a string of one generation within two generations that are separated, Father and Son. If you want to talk about seventeen years of Chinese history [as I did in this film] you have to deal with two strings. Otherwise you can't show it clearly. If you just took up the Father's string it would be heavy and oppressive. It would be like you were writing politics, a nation's developments, a nation's characteristics. You see, I think that in those seventeen years children, although they were suppressed, that those children were still kind of empty, they occupied a space that was not developing at the same pace as adults. So making two spaces in one film, gives the audience a kind of warm feeling. (Tian, Beijing 1999)

In other parts of the same interview Tian is very critical of the work of the Children's Film Studio, arguing that only children could really make children's films that they might enjoy. In this he echoes several interviewees of his own and the present "sixth" generation who are disappointed with the state of children's film. Some even complained that their own children watched "too much" television because films were so hard to come by. Tian makes less of a personal issue from the problem and more a statement about the rights of children to determine their entertainment values. He is completely supportive of the agency of children, and in the idea that children's media should be made by children for children in the best of possible worlds. Here, however, he seems much closer in perspective to his mother than he perhaps realised. The strings of his film rely on a sympathetic engagement between the adult past and a child's memory. Between them they elicit empathy in the audience. The human feeling that a film like *Heavenly Letter* strives to demonstrate for its young audiences, is also central to the structure—literally the structure of feeling—that Tian has created for his adult film about history, politics, and adult failure. The string (*yi tiaoxian*)— of the kite—that pulls together father and son is not so far away from the letter on the kite string bonding the grandfather with the little boy in *Heavenly Letter*. When Yu Lan makes a leap from a question about political stability and children's media to a reminiscence about her own troubled childhood and the defining moment of her identity, she is not doing anything very dissimilar from her son's cinematic rendition of two spaces, the heavy politics of the adult world and the search of a child and a young woman for the defining moment of consciousness. Both the character in the film and Yu Lan herself opted for resistance.

If *ganqing* is part of the publicness of children's media, providing the thread of communication between one age and another, there is yet some notion of harmony within hierarchy in contemporary China. That is the optimistic outlook to which Studio workers hold fast. What justifications are there, however, for an optimistic account of the recent past, as it impacts on the present time? Does this outlook on contemporary history imply old-fashioned nostalgia, and a privileging of tired genres and old relationships? The argument here does not pretend that *Heavenly Letter* is a great film, nor that it can create a lasting, contemporary "sense of belonging to a larger whole." Rather, I argue that its intentions, those of its makers and distributors, embody not only a residual impulse to socialism and the centralised organization of people's relationships and socialisation, but also a belief in belonginess that belies the fatalism of commentaries on reform China. The film demonstrates a strong, and to this viewer somewhat misogynistic, mistrust for the generation of reform (the "mother" in the film) whose grasp of children's emotional welfare is slim. Human feeling is predicated on their return to the wider family base——old and young——and therefore to a socialised "harmony within hierarchy," rather than a market-orientated relationship with other people.

The film's appeal to the older generation as a repository of feeling (*gan-qing*) for the young is not a secret. Chen Baoguang, a Senior Fellow of the Chinese Film Art Society, has admitted quite candidly that some children's films are for children and some are about older people's memories of being children.[11] This trend is visible in many productions. Older people act as mediators between children and disturbed, deracinated, or dysfunctional parents. In *I Am a Fish* (*wo shi yitiao yu* 2002) a small boy—also brought up by his grandfather—seeks to contact him after his death by swimming to greet him (the grandfather has convinced him that fishermen become fish after their deaths). Again the parents are inadequate. They want the boy to live in the city, to do well at school, to conform to sociality as defined by modern standards of individual achievement. They cannot provide emotional feeling, harmony, or stable hierarchies for his general well-being. At an early screening the film received some criticism for not emphasising school as a positive influence in the boy's life, but the young director—supported by older studio executive workers—resisted this criticism. Children, he says, deserve to explore the fantasy world that supports love, fear, and grief, they deserve to live beyond politics but within a world that acknowledges the challenges that they face in a modernising and competitive environment. The morality in this tale is not functional, it is affective. School has nothing to do with it.[12]

The little boy in *I Am a Fish* is not a comedian nor a puppet, but the character also represents a notion of value that exceeds the competencies of education and fitting the norm. Li Honghe's film has been praised in the press for achieving what other children's film lack—the element of fantasy that binds children and adults together in cultural adventure. The studio, and children's films in general, are otherwise criticised for not understanding the imperatives of market response. This understanding is partly about commercial sense, and partly about an imagination, which encompasses and extends the contemporary public imagination. It requires a level of cinematic creativity to lift a film from explicit educational functionality and stark morality tales to subtlety. One Beijing critic gave the example of the English author Philip Pullman's trilogy, *His Dark Materials*, as books that transcend boundaries between adult and child tastes, and which do so by daring to challenge adult beliefs of good and evil.[13] The critic could have added that Pullman draws on cultural memories in his adult/parent readers too. Every English-speaking reader who has been close to the Tolkien trilogy, Herbert Read's *The Green Child* (1935), C. S. Lewis's Narnia series, and the Proppist morphologies of the folk and fairy tale will know that they are being addressed by Pullman as sophisticated members of a cultural trajectory, as adults and as children in a web of morality, education, and religious power in an adult world.

Pullman offers a repudiation of God that places the lives of children and the love of adults as the most powerful forces in the worlds he creates. He destroys myths but he maintains the thread of human feeling (*ganqing*) to keep the books and his characters alive. Likewise, the same critic notes that the fantasy element in *I Am a Fish* succeeds in part because of the central relationship between grandfather and boy: "The boy and his grandfather had a deep bond between them. His Grandfather told him: when people die, they turn into a fish" ("*ta dui yeye you hen shen de ganqing. Yeye gen ta shou, ren si hou hui biaocheng yiytiao yu*") (Yu X. 2002, 123). Without *ganqing*, there can be no believable communication between the old and the young, and no chance, in this particular story, that a boy might try to become a fish and follow his grandfather into the spirit world. Films that are too self-conscious in talking only to children, and for children, miss the subtlety that attracts audiences across the generations. What is more, as every children's film-maker knows, if you cannot lure the parents into the cinema it will be much harder to get them to bring their children.

The "modernising and competitive environment" is not kind to films that fail; but their narrative intentions need to be noted before their distribution channels dry up completely. They are, after all, part of the cultural expression of the reform era, every bit as much as the adoption of Macworld food and toys, English Disney on VCD, and Pokémon stickers. *Heavenly Letter* has not made a serious commercial impact. It is available on VCD through a television company, but was not mentioned by a single student in three years of surveys of favourite media product. However, for a significant generation of parents, grandparents, and media workers it expresses something about human feeling (*ganqing*) that escapes the clean break versions of reform. There is a tendency in cultural critique worldwide to focus on the new, and therefore emphasise the trajectory of (post-) modernisation over other narratives of cultural production. This discussion hopes to place a very small pebble back on the scales of historical memory.

NEW DIRECTIONS

Responses to political, economic, and social change as they are evinced in children's media in the PRC may be categorised as educational, affective, market-oriented, and morally functional. The affective mode is most often used in live action film made by the Children's Film Studio. The overtly information-led educational productions appear more often on television. There are also shows made specifically for educational deployment (usually in environmental projects and in learning English).

Both modes of address, affective and educational, tend towards moral functionality, but only television manages to combine this with the economic possibilities of the child market, especially of course through its advertising slots. The growth of television for children is currently a matter for market watchers to judge. Anecdotally the growth and the whispers of co-production growth are great. Shanghai TV and Shanghai animation studios are now in the same mega production house. Southern Star, an Australian television company with Beijing Film Academy educated producers, is involved in China-Australia co-productions (*Magic Mountain* screens on the Australian Broadcasting Authority children's slot for preschoolers). Large British-owned production houses such as Pearson are reportedly cutting deals with CCTV. Disney is certainly involved in the distribution of its merchandise and character animations across the CCTV network. Home-grown productions are also beginning to rival the popularity of Taiwanese teen soaps.[14] Li Shaohong's vaguely historical *Princess* series was hugely popular in 1999–2000. Li is a fifth generation film-maker whose classic women's film *Blush* enjoyed a gala screening at the London Film Festival in 1992, and whose production company has its base in the Beijing Film Studios compound. Her temporary migration to television suggests that the cost flexibility and reportedly gentler censorship systems for broadcast television make working in the medium attractive. Likewise Peng Xiaolian, also a fifth generation graduate, and winner of an early Golden Calf award for *Me and My Classmates* (*Wo he wode tongxue* 1987), was in 2001–2003 working on a part live action, part animation children's television series for Shanghai,[15] although it was never properly distributed.

Film-makers and television directors of this calibre make the future of home-produced television look promising. They have already proved that they can work across the categories of media acceptability in a Chinese media sphere, without compromising subtlety or intelligence. The film-makers-turned-television directors offer Chinese children's media the best hope in an increasingly internationalised televisual world. "New" media and "new" communications worldwide have developed, multiplied, and proliferated at a rate that has defined modernity across many, very different places. Space and time, as Anthony Giddens (1990) and many others have argued,[16] have been collapsed, extended, and digitised by a number of technologies and applications. The nature and speed of these phenomena have in part been determined by the localisation of media forms and content, and also by the ongoing texture of everyday life in particular places. If, for example, we acknowledge that children in almost all developed English-speaking communicative zones, including much of Asia, have accessed and enjoyed *Toy Story* (Pixar/Disney),[17] *The Lion King* (Disney), and *Mulan* (Disney) the questions remain: What have they made of it? How have the fantasy structures enacted in the movie impacted on their sense of self? Are these borrowed stories, off-the-shelf fantasies of somewhere entirely different? Or are they as much a fantasy of the pleasures of reform, as *Heavenly Letter* is a fantasy of the return of collective intergenerational virtue?

In pursuing these questions with child audiences in China it has appeared that the socialisation and educative imperatives, that Chinese adults and media professionals discuss as an essential part of the process of reception, actually work. As I discuss in chapter 4, children responded in relation to their media use in three interconnecting veins. They were creative, cosmopolitan, and local. These competencies were rooted in a schema of values that tied in with the educational imperative sought by their elders. The choices that they made in order to explore these values were, however, not necessarily domestically produced. The creation of the Studio in 1981, to preserve a socialised succession for the future, may be judged to have both failed and succeeded. It was an institutional response to a social problem, its research arm followed three years after its inception. One could question why the research into problems of children's media did not precede the solution. The easy answer is that politics had to be seen to be done, and then shown to have been effective by research. The institutional response is both a convenient way of managing the visibility of political action, within an existing network of state-sponsored activity. The institution is a determined form of socialised creative application and as such does not spawn anything unexpected.

This is not to say that the Studio is not an interesting phenomenon. Its productions are occasionally affective, if not wildly popular. They do build social competency and they also contribute to an expectation that children's media should be a national priority. There are also some unplanned outcomes. The Studio was established to create a media source for children that was morally healthy, and which would work to build appropriate successors to the current generation of Party faithful. It was, however, also effective in career rehabilitation and in the development and testing of new talent. Film workers could regain their faith in their careers, building a relationship between an ageing cultural élite and a strange, modernising generation of young people. They could move between film school and television whilst practising film skills in a subsidised studio (one of the very few to persist).

The élite still exists much as it did twenty years ago, but the young audience has grown and been replaced by two more generations of modern Chinese consumers. The fear that prompted the studio initiative, that the culture of social propriety and revolutionary succession would fail, seems to have been realised. Where the Studio has failed is in the market end of media distribution and exhibition. The merchandising take-up of the *Blue Cat* (*lanmao*) on television underwrites the production of videos and VCDs of children's studio films. A few titles make it into audiovisual stores on this basis. Yet the Studio does not merchandise its own characters, and there is little evidence of sales strategies and marketing tie-ins elsewhere on the networks or in the toy stores. CCTV6 screens their films occasionally, but prefers to look back to the "classics" when discussing children's film as a notable part of cinematic culture.[18] In any case, CCTV6 is a subscription movie channel and does not attract child audiences who are interested in cartoons on Channel 7, or teenagers who watch the Taiwanese soapies in prime time.

The entire enterprise of the Studio is predominantly funded by a reward system, whereby ten children's films a year compete for seven hundred thousand RMB worth of governmental subsidy, under the Golden Calf Award scheme. Altogether the state subsidises children's film up to one-and-one-half million RMB per annum. This level of support demonstrates that the socialisation initiative of the early 1980s continues. Socialisation is not, however, the liberal democratic U.S. version somewhat ironised by Norma Pecora. Whilst the Love Children Society seeks corporate sponsorship for distribution, there is not yet the sense that children's film has really leveraged the financial advantages of advertisement and tie-ins. Children are, if you like, still a bit precious in film, although not at all in television.[19] Pecora suggests that U.S. children have long been socialised as good, brand-aware consumers, associating Ronald McDonald with "good things."

> When television was established in the mid 1950s, children continued to be an important market for these goods [cereals and candy] while experts argued children should be given the freedom to make their own decisions and—a boon to advertisers. Children were now seen as more self-sufficient in purchasing decisions . . . the idea was that if they could be attracted to a product at a young age, they would remain loyal customers when they became older and "real" consumers. (Pecora 1998, 20)

This doubtful moral system is certainly not that evangelised by the Studio. However, motivated by political anxiety, and thereby doomed to only limited success, a subsidisation of children's Party-led civility is not the answer to the film industry's need for an audience. The Studio encapsulates the international experience of adults in the face of media content for children. They both make films and distrust their potential. The media are seen as a resource to be exploited for implicit and explicit socialisation and ideological training for the young. They are also feared as potential corrupters of children, mistrusted as distractions for the reproduction of social order and moral development to which children's education and family life aspires.

NOTES

1. See Poshek Fu for an alternative genealogy of Chinese film that prioritises Southern Chinese, Shanghai, and Hong Kong film-making (Fu 2003).

2. Recollected in Yu Lan's Preface (*qian yan*), "A Small Cheering Squad," (*yige xiaoxiao de lala dui*) to the tenth anniversary celebratory booklet of the Children's Film Association, 1994.

3. A complete list of film titles from 1981–2001 is available from the author.

4. Winner of the eighth Golden Rooster award and the eleventh Hundred Flowers Award for her role as Duan Xifeng in *Old Well* (co-starring with Zhang Yimou). She is also known internationally for her appearance in *The Blue Kite* and *Crouching Tiger, Hidden Dragon* (Ang Lee 2000)   ·

5. Publicity notes.

6. Anonymous interviewee, Beijing Film Studio, 2000.

7. Interview at Xie Tian's home, November 1998. At the time of writing this book (2003) Xie Tian was very sick in hospital. He was eighty-eight years old. He died in December 2003.

8. Xie Tian did manage to make it back onto film in the 1940s, mainly through the good offices of Tian Fang, Yu Lan's husband, director of the Beijing Film studio.

9. Further discussions of questionnaires and focus groups are given in chapters 3 and 4.

10. See reference to this discussion with Tian in Donald (2000).

11. Interview, Beijing, July 2002. "There are two kinds of children's films, one is naïve for young children. These make children happy and reflect their lives. The other kind is that wherein adults recall their childhoods; the adults extract meaning from children's lives. The latter is profound and the art level is higher—but adults never appreciate films that really young children enjoy."

12. Interview with Li Honghe, Beijing, July 2002.

13. Yu (2001).

14. *Yongyuan de lantian* (*Blue Sky Forever*) was the big favourite in 2001.

15. Source: *Screen Digest* 2002.

16. Paraphrased in (Kapur 1999, 129) as "the continuous questioning of old knowledge and replacement with new data are basic features of the reflexivity inherent in modernity itself."

17. Conservative projections in 1996 were video sales of thirty million outside the United States (Pixar website).

18. CCTV 6 hosted a discussion of children's film in July 2002. Sixty percent of the airtime was taken up with retrospective, and the rest debating why children's film was no longer vibrant. Unfavourable comparisons were made between *Babe* and the productions of the Children's Film Studio.

19. At 22 percent, China has the third fastest growth in advertising expenditure worldwide. Source: *Screen Digest*.

3

"Messengers" or Consumers? Children in Children's Film

Baseball Boy *(dir. Qi Jian 2002) won the Golden Calf (Tongniu)[1] award for the best Chinese (Mainland) children's feature in 2002. The film is a good example of the negotiation between old and new value systems as they are expressed in the culture of children's entertainment. The story features characters and themes that are familiar from earlier periods of children's film: the quintessential naughty but heroic boy figure, a committed teacher: (here a baseball coach torn between the schoolboy team and promotion to a league club), and an overriding national trajectory of sporting success against adversity. Whilst these characters are generic, their context is quite new. The major dramatic impulse is the tension between domestic and national interests: family and team loyalties, individual profit, and collective endeavour, but the resolution of the drama is a negotiation between these aspects of a contemporary child's life. It is thus a film that draws heavily on past models whilst attempting "edutainment" for the youth of 2002. The conciliatory movement of the plot's resolution is reminiscent of* Ah Cradle! *and the value of human feeling evident in that earlier text.*

The film begins with a tussle over real estate as a baseball pitch used by an amateur boys' team is redeveloped as a soccer field to please local property owners, one of whom is a team member's father. The boy in question is also having trouble with his performance on the field. He is unable to commit himself physically to the game, mainly, we come to realise, because without the support of his father, he is not fully enabled to achieve his potential. As the family and the team sort out their differences, the boy improves his game and becomes a key striker. Through his efforts the team gets into the Junior Asian Games, but he cannot go as he has broken his leg in the semi-finals. The film ends with a heroic stance by the wounded boy; the

49

last shot pulling out on an image of him standing on the reclaimed baseball pitch. This same shot sets the boy against a huge national flag, which covers the entire sports ground, whilst a text rolls over the credits describing the film's young heroes as future Olympic champions in 2008. The penultimate sequence shows the boy and his father playing soccer together in their family garden.

This chapter discusses the ways in which children are depicted in the media and the extent to which their role as successors to the national project is now viewed through a lens of consumerism and capital. It suggests that children are in the foreground of the mediated debate on the relationship between being a Chinese citizen and a national subject in the PRC, and being a player in the new economy.

In *Baseball Boy* the discussion revolves easily around the drive to profit and the need to stand up as a sporting nation. The emphasis on national pride and sporting success is to be expected in the run up to 2008——and especially as the film was shot and edited in 2002, the year in which Beijing moved seriously into its Olympic preparations. Thus, as the State capitalises on its newfound internationalism by winning the global competition for the Olympics, the characters in the film are faced with the anomalies of national capitalism. The entrepreneurial imperative that defines much new Chinese business practice is acknowledged in the characterisation of the boy's father. With some foresight, in the year in which China failed to qualify for the second round in the World Cup, a film succeeds in portraying soccer as a destructive infiltrator in China's "real" sports hopes, but also acknowledges that it is popular. The boy and his dad still get to play a game in the garden. Meanwhile, the baseball pitch becomes a battleground of local team spirit, and, when the boys win through to the regional championships, of national sporting pride. The father figure, enmeshed in real estate deals, is set up as a new adversary to replace the 1930s Shanghai mobsters in *Sanmao*, and the 1940s Japanese aggressors and Nationalist Party "traitors" in *Zhangga* and *Shanshan*. Now, although the seeming aggressor is also motivated by forces of capital, land appropriation, and profit, his final integration and recuperation is necessary to the story's happy ending. He is, after all, the father of a team member. This gives the narrative a different job to that of ousting the enemy. It sets out to achieve the reclamation of the quasi-capitalist into a mutual and coherent national view.

Capital operates therefore as a structural device in the plot representing destructive "outside" intervention, but one that is also finally susceptible to good local persuasion; its ill effects can be overridden by improved family relationships and better communications between the generations. The development of the team is predicated on the development of a good understanding between a boy and his father, and therefore between team spirit and the ambitions of capital interests. The plotting draws on familiar aspects of national character developed within the film, to earn the harmony at the end. The son demonstrates physical bravery, finally breaking a leg as he learns to dive on the pitch, and the coach also shows moral integrity, by putting the team's interests before his own career. Finally even the father combines his own money-oriented morality with a different, softer take on real estate. He is still living off capital rather than labour, but he is now using it for the good of the team, the microcosm of the nation. By the end of the film the boy and his father are very much together (playing soccer in the garden at home), and the sports coach is working to build an honourable if less glitzy career with his young charges as they prepare to represent China at the Asia Games in Korea. The father has been redeemed by his acknowledgment of his love for his son, and the coach has been validated by the achievement of his team.

The redemptive moment in Chinese film has been noted by Esther Yau. It is a violent and only selectively forgiving component of revolutionary filmmaking (Yau 1990). Redemption is still at work in this negotiated narrative, overlaid and underpinned by clear political messages of national togetherness, family stability, and selflessness. The enemy is a different beast now, open to negotiation, and susceptible to family emotion. The film may not do well at an open box office in competition with *Finding Nemo* (Pixar 2003), but watching this film in a (free-of-charge) crowded children's screening in Zibo it was clear that the deployment of the national flag was well understood within the fantasy structure of the young audience's imaginations. The flag meshed with the story of modern development and family tensions, symbolising success on all fronts, both for the protagonists and their local spectators. Writing about children's representation in political posters of the 1960s and 1970s I have argued that they are used as political messengers (Donald 1999). In this film children are still political messengers, now bringing home the possibility of social stability moving hand-in-hand with private development and international sporting success.

CHILDREN'S DAY

On Children's Day 2000, thousands of Beijing schoolchildren crowded into Tiananmen Square to celebrate and be photographed. Millions more across the city and the nation performed in school shows for their families and friends. Others went with their parents to parks, to the zoo, to the cinema, and to the aquarium. Many went shopping to take advantage of Children's Day sales and special offers. It was a media feast. For several days running up to Children's Day and on the day itself, the press was full of stories of children—their successes, their relationship to busy working parents, their importance to the economy, and their role as symbols of and successors to the nation's future.

Children's Day, otherwise known as 1 June (*liu yi*), is an international holiday celebrated on different dates in various parts of the world.[2] In China the
day is perhaps more passionately and widely celebrated than are European
and American equivalents. It is an annual example of the nation's seriousness and consistency in the symbolic management of children's place in the
nation. Whilst it is not surprising that schools should be active in promoting
this festival, the extent of mainstream media coverage suggests a deeper connection between the idea of childhood and the underlying principles of social and political life in China.

On 1 June 2001 and 2002, the *People's Daily* and the *China Daily* both carried full-colour images of children dancing in formation in Tiananmen
Square. These images were institutional and intensely nationalistic, the children were representing schools and culture palaces across the capital. The
dances and gymnastic displays were similar in scale and precision to the military formations of National Day (1 October), which occupy the same space
at the physical centre of state power.

Yet the advertising columns in the newspapers also carried short features
on shopping opportunities, debates on children's relationships with single
parents, and suggestions where parents and children should go to enjoy the
holiday. The festival of children's rights in a socialist political economy had
begun the transition to being also a festival of consumption marked by advertisement and blanket media coverage. This transition exemplifies the
shift to market-driven capitalist enterprise in China, with children as an
emerging focus of the economy in general, and the advertising industry in
particular. As China's media are changing under the impact of globalisation,
new technologies, and the emergence of the sophisticated and demanding
consumer, so China's children epitomise this emerging consumer. They collectively embody China's economic future, educated as moral, national subjects, for whom international consumption is, ideally, a necessary way of
supporting China's successful entry into the world economic system. Commentators on China's media have described the "globalization of thought
work" (Lynch 1999), and the maturing of thought work into "spectacular
self-representation" towards "a sophisticated reproduction of nationalist
ideology resituated in the new consumerism of emerging middle-class
China." (Lee 2003, 55) and "the impression of pluralism without creating
scenarios that directly criticise the leadership of the CCP" (Keane 2003, 182).
Undoubtedly children's media are crucial elements of this process of sophisticated smoke and mirrors.

It is important, however, to recognise that films are more than just a tech-
nique of economic politicisation. They also tell stories that speak to children
about the rapid changes in the world they inhabit. *Baseball Boy* and Children's Day are both products of an integrated system of socialisation, seek-
ing to produce children as model, moral citizens. They are also products of

the early twenty-first century, needing to work cultural magic for consumers and for the state. Even as *Baseball Boy* picks up the Golden Calf award, the Love Children Society is working desperately to find charitable and corporate sponsors for its distribution. Economic realities pose a notable difference between the challenges for a children's film in 2002 and the relatively straightforward remit of Maoist era culture. Likewise, Children's Day is still a state-sponsored event, but one which makes sense increasingly in commercial terms as much as in its contribution to the national character. A number one primary school in Beijing ran two events at its Children's Day Festival in 2000: a fashion parade with children wearing designer clothes, followed by a choir singing a paean to the courage of the model soldier, Lei Feng. The audience reacted most warmly to the first item.

By contrast with the need to sponsor film distribution in 2002, classic products of the 1960s were screened by dictate, and not in competition with international blockbusters and formatted television shows. The animated classic and picture book, *Little Sisters of the Grasslands*, tells the story of two Mongolian minority (*Menggu minzu*) girls, the sisters Lungmei and Yurong. They are depicted as brave and loyal children who rescue a lost goat in a blizzard, putting their own lives in danger to do so. In the picture book version the children are shown first at a study meeting, learning the couplet: Listen to the words of Chairman Mao/Follow in the footsteps of the Communist Party (*ting Mao zhuxi hua, gen gongchan dang zou*). In the film, the enduring image is of the elder sister carrying her little sister on her back to save her from frostbite. As they struggle through the driving snow, their father and community leaders ride out in a posse to carry them back to a (perfectly white) hospital where the young heroines recover. The story serves several political functions. It emphasises both the courage and hardiness of Mongolian ethnicity (for a discussion, see Khan and Riskin 2001) but also reiterates the need to recuperate all minority children into a wider national narrative (Hansen 1999). The sisters are finally saved by the modern medicine and hygienic facilities provided by the hospital, a symbol of the modernity brought by Han interventions in Mongolia.

The film is dramatic, but has no real dramatic tension embedded in the characters or the relationships between them. It is rather all about harmony in the face of natural adversity. There is no disharmony between the sisters, in the tribal community where they live, nor between community leaders, doctors, and other children. This underlines the focus on national integration at all costs. Lungmei and Yujong were produced as models (*mofan*) for other children to emulate. In particular their role is to demonstrate that one can be both a bold Mongolian and a true Chinese national whatever the circumstances. Child models were regularly developed in school textbooks, comic books, and on film. Based on real-life exemplars, the child models were often tragic figures. Although the Little Sisters made it home with the help of their community, many child models were feted and promulgated for their willingness to die for their politico-national loyalty. The political expectations that these children fulfilled were focused on internal morality manifested through physical courage in the service of an integrated community and Party-state.

In 2002, there is a shift. Suffering is still heroic but it is constrained by normal circumstance (the boy hurts his leg) and social relationships are complex. Whilst the national Olympian theme is clear in *Baseball Boy*, nevertheless the film has to admit to domestic disharmony within a single family, (even if this is resolved by the end of the film). Although seemingly a very "safe" film in political attitudes, *Baseball Boy* is also part of a wedge in Chinese cinema, admitting to the complex social attitudes that arise in response to a market economy.

In *Baseball Boy* the boys achieve collective greatness and individual improvement, but they are not "models" in the sense of the 1960s and 1970s characterisations. They model some appropriate and some inappropriate behaviour in difficult situations, but their association with national priorities are qualitatively different to revolutionary martyrs. These lads are more in the tradition of Sanmao and Zhangga than Shanshan. They learn to *manage* situations through intelligent compromise as well as through persistence, and their emotional ties are complex rather than suicidal. In model stories, children plunge into an abyss of frenetic goodness and sacrifice. Their emotional commitment is based on trauma rather than survival. In the present era, there is a remodelled return of intelligent initiative in the name of survival and profit on the one hand, and ordinary happiness on the other: the child figure, which has retained the strongest presence in the contemporary field of representation is the feisty creation of the 1930s. Sanmao's dramatic motivation was to outsmart anyone richer than himself so he might eat. Zhangga joined the revolutionary cause to revenge his slain grandmother—but also because he really wanted to play with a real gun. They were boys first and social revolutionaries second. One might go further and suggest that the trickster comic character of Sanmao is himself derivative of the classic trickster figure, Monkey King (*sun wukung*). Along this trajectory one can also see the traces of Monkey in popular Japanese animated characters, particularly the transformers and Pikachu from the Pokémon series, but also in American animation, where the "stretched and squashed" Mickey Mouse and friends are also capable of visual trickery and shape shifting. From this perspective, it can be argued that Chinese characterisations are rejoining a mainstream of children's favourites to which they made significant early contributions.

The status of children themselves is similarly complex, in traditional and revolutionary media forms (Anagnost 1997; Farquhar 1999; Behnke Kinney 1995; Laing 1996; Landsberger 1995). Anagnost has made interesting connections between social change and children as creative consumers, a point which allows that children are both active participants in the modern world, and exemplars of the way in which capital is activated. Farquhar has written the definitive history of revolutionary print media, noting the shift from Confucian pedagogy to educative social comment and the idea of literature in the 1920s and 1930s, into hard-line moral education after 1949. Again she shows that children are addressed both as agents of their own media use, but also as moral receptacles of adult hopes for present and future. Laing and Landsberger write from the perspectives of art history on the one hand, and sociopolitical description on the other. Both discover images of play and family, which also serve a larger narrative of social self-description.

There is also a tangible and sympathetic sense of children's social value in any discussion that touches on childhood in China. Whereas Landsberger, for instance, argues that images of children are only serving the requirements of direct political indoctrination (Landsberger 2001), the picture is less clearcut, children are indeed political messengers, but ones which also carry a real affective weight of hope for older generations. Studies of the concept of childhood in China quote early discussion of the value of a child's life in direct relation to and tension with official responsibilities, of the sorrow of parting from an infant, and of the social responsibility that the rich bear to the poor in respect to the care of the young:

> The growing tendency to write about children with deep affection probably began with the ninth century. The case of Han Yu (768–824) . . . was typical. . . . His fourth daughter, Na, died en route [to the family's banishment] and was hastily buried. [He later wrote]: "When I travelled back from the south I could see your eyes and face. How could I ever forget your words and expressions?" (Wu 1995, 138–39)

Mary Farquhar has shown that much more recent literature also contains an awareness of children as a cohort of social significance and affective power. Her analysis of Lu Xun's short fiction demonstrates how words could evoke the underlying image of childishness and vulnerability and be then employed in the service of the 4 May modern tendency, and as a hook for wider political statements. "Lu Xun's schema was explicit. Parents must first understand children and their world [*ertong shijie*] so as not to hinder children's development. . . . Children . . . often imagine the world, beyond the moon and the stars . . . they imagine flying into the sky and burrowing into an ant's nest" (Farquhar 1999, 60–63).

Children are routinely portrayed as the hope, brightness, stars, flowers, and future of China. This is not particular either to the reform or the revolutionary eras, but there are differences in emphasis. In revolutionary periods, virtue was linked through the figure of the child to a wider political optimism. The ubiquitous representation, narrative frequency, and overwhelming media presence of children helped the Party to define the values underlying the processes of socialisation. Films from the 1950s (*Flowers of the Motherland* [*zuguo de huarduo*], 1955) 1960s (*Flower Garden*, 1962), and

1970s (*Sparkling Red Star* [*Shanshan hongxing*]) use metaphors of flowering, light, and hope to frame political and social fables for family consumption. Similarly, in posters of the time, children embody better relations with Taiwan, succour for PLA soldiers, and a general belief that the revolutionary past can forge a revolutionary future (Donald 1999; Landsberger 1995; 2001). Currently, in the print media, especially on key dates such as Children's Day, children have news value but it is taken as intrinsic to their value as children rather than their role as revolutionary models. They are still headlined as the "repository of the future" and the basis for all worthwhile human development (Huang et al. 2000, 47), but that is not immediately tied to an undifferentiated version of moral goodness. Rather, they are mobile proto-citizens who will be trained to manage any moral, physical, and intellectual demands that the new society might bring into play. The contemporary follow-on of revolutionary childhoods has needed to incorporate the new in the discourse of the old:

> Education must serve the socialist modernization drive and must be combined with production and physical labour in order to train for the socialist cause builders and successors who are developed in an all-round way—morally, intellectually, and physically. (Article 5, The Education Law of China PRC 1995)

Or, as the Research Institute into Children and Teenagers (2000) puts it, children are products of the reform, but also creators of the new ways. It is not that they have no ideological position or aims in life, but that they do not make false claims on their thinking, they combine a doable expectation of the self with a realistic attitude to the development of society (152–53). They are self-directed but also participants (*zizhu he canyu*) in a wider story of national progress. In 2000 the Institute reported research into five thousand primary and middle school children in Beijing municipality (urban and rural) to find out how they described their priorities. Nearly 20 percent (19.43 percent) opted for "intellectual knowledge" (*zhishi*), 17.6 percent chose "employment" (*shiye*), 14.41 percent chose "material comforts" (*wuzhi xiangshou*), 11.86 percent wanted an "individual sense of virtue and morality" (*geren daode*), 10.43 percent wanted "freedom" (*ziyou*), and 4.89 percent prioritised family relationships (*jiating guanxi*) (152ff). With these kinds of attitudes prevailing amongst youth, it seems that over the coming years, Children's Day will be celebrating an increasingly diverse population of ideals and aspirations.

QUALITY AND RIGHTS

The pragmatic outcome of children's "all round" education is conceptualised in the system as a "quality" (*suzhi*) appropriate to modern living. Children's intellectual, moral, and physical development combines to produce quality, which betters the children's personal futures and in turn supports a national agenda to build quality amongst the citizenry as a whole. Quality as an outcome of socialisation is taught in schools through the national curriculum—the same curriculum that forbids Disney English in the classroom, but which, in the Film Course, encourages children to appreciate *Bambi* (for a fuller discussion of the Film Course, see chapter 4). Quality is also supported by wealthy and aspirant parents who will pay large sums to maintain their children's access to new technologies, to excellent tertiary entrance results, and to English as a second language. At the other end of the economic scale, many children are economically useful to their families, but cannot access the quality represented by all-round education. Children still work in poorer areas of the country, and a reported one million children a year "drop out" before finishing primary school. Despite stated state-level commitment to bring education to the rural poor, locally disbursed monies are less effective in poorer areas where parents cannot make up the difference between basic and modern education resources (Khan and Riskin 2001). In addition to the needs of poor families, there are the problems of deracinated domestic migrants, and ongoing inequities between provincial and county level initiatives (Tsang 2001; Beemer 2001).

In the late 1980s, the controversial film *Childhood in Ruijin* (1989, *Tongnian zai Ruijin*) dealt head on with the problems facing rural children wanting to attend school but unable to avoid work. In the film, six children study together to complete their homework in an apparent rural idyll of perseverance and communal self-help. One by one, however, the children are forced out of school by life circumstances: namely parental poverty, and an overweaning rural prejudice against girls' education. The same theme dominates *Ice Flower* (*Lubinghua*, Taiwan 1989), also popular on the Mainland, Zhang Yimou's *Not One Less* (*Yige ye bu neng shao* 1999) and the Nanjing Studio's *Thatched Memories* (*Cao fangzi* 2001). These films are all at pains to deliver the message that childhood should be a period for learning in a safe environment, characterised as "school." However, all the films admit that this environment is variable. Intellectual, moral, and physical development is dependent on the financial security of one's parents, and the attitudes of society. The photograph of four orphans "adopted" by the Geng Changsuo collective in 1953 (Friedman, Pickowicz, and Selden 1991, 110) offers documentation of a hoped-for social responsibility. These recent films' concentration on rural tragedies is less optimistic. They underline the new reform dichotomies of quality and modernisation: rural and urban, rich and poor, super-educated and subeducated. The compulsory nine years of education, announced in 1985 and 1993, is vastly differentiated between public and private schools, urban and rural, east and western provinces. In minority areas, the "nine years" directives were diluted to a projection of six years by 2000

(Hansen 1999, 22). Poorer sections of society value their children as much as the grief-stricken mandarin Han Yu, but are pushed to cover essential living costs, apart from education. The *Little Sisters of the Grasslands* nearly died rescuing a goat. In the mindset of the 1960s' era of model children, they were ideal schoolchildren, combining work and learning in a commitment to community and Maoist principles. From the perspective of *Childhood in Ruijin*, it is accepted that children who go to work do not go to school, and children who don't get educated are missing out on the rights to the "quality" of the new Chinese citizen.

One expectation under the rubric of "rights" is that children do not sell their labour in any substantial way until they have reached their mid to late teens.[3] In a developed economy, as Zelizer has asserted in a U.S. context, children are "economically useless but emotionally priceless" (Zelizer 1998, 82). Zelizer's comment arises from her work on children's labour in pre-war America, and on subsequent generations who do not work (or do not work legally).[4] She points to the connection between children and the media sphere as one that is characterised by consumer behaviour, but that the consumers are themselves material icons of the economy in which they grow. They are "priceless" because they are "useless"—living symbols of a developed world that can afford to keep its children out of the workforce for a long period of time. This time is called childhood, and the exploitation of child labour is condemned as a betrayal of childhood itself. It hardly needs saying that in China children are also priceless. The betrayal of childhood is a slight on the happiness of the young but also on the continuation of a family, and its modern macro-counterpart, the nation. In a survey on children and television, over 58 percent of adults knew about the "Convention on the Rights of the Child" and 94 percent knew of the Chinese extrapolation, the "Law for the Protection of Minors." The authors of the survey attribute this to a central plank of media responsibility: "To show that the government cares for children is a main task of Chinese media" (Huang et al. 2000, 50).

The sample for Huang's study of child rights was urban and relatively affluent. Nevertheless, similar research has suggested that the "Law for the Protection of Minors" is widely known in China, and indeed helps people define childhood when questioned.[5] Children are legally visible then in the popular imagination, and as such are figures of great importance in the communicative sphere, which supports that imagination. As the films under discussion suggest, children appear in media in terms that are affective but also which underlie their role in the future of China as a nation. In the former role they are subject to, and subjects of, sentiment, emotion, and iconic *description*. In the latter category of political propaganda and public communications, children's presence builds in a sense of *succession*; of children taking the present struggles into future happiness and national success. These two roles meld together in the media of advertisement. In the late 1990, and there have been more recent arguments supporting this (Jing Wang 2001; 2004), children continue to be significant in advertisements as a means of grounding international brands in a local affectivity to resonate with children's place in society. As in political posters children were used to ground Maoism in a recognisable and emotive reality, so in modern communications they assume the iconic *responsibility* for the succession of Chineseness, of national goals, and of particular political formations in the era of reform.

CONTROL AND SOCIALISATION

The transfer of children's iconic effect from politics to commerce sometimes appears seamless, and from that stems arguments such as Landsberger's (1995), that claim a peculiar and totalising control over the image of the child in Chinese media. Anxiety as a characteristic of adult/child relations is, however, well demonstrated in debates on the media worldwide. Those that produce media for children are often mistrusted for their motivations—as in the U.K. furor over the "babyishness" of *Teletubbies* (a pre-school program!), the U.S. panic over "witchcraft" and anti-Christian sentiment in *Harry Potter*, and Chinese educationalists' worries about pornography in girl adventure animation from Japan. When children commit acts of violence, their media consumption is blamed first (Barker and Petley 1997). Meanwhile, there are rather few initiatives that see media as a positive force, which may support as well as undermine morality and intellectual development. When adults debate children's media (created and financed, after all, by adults themselves), they do so with a level of anxiety that prompts them to seek pre-emptive control of children's media use. In looking at Chinese media for children, and the figure of the child as it appears in Chinese media more generally, it is fair to remember that adults the world over seek a rationale for their need to take charge of children's images and imaginations in this area.

Wartella has argued that in the United States, although children's media have been researched mainly in relation to their uses and subsequent (ill) effects, this has occurred in a wider context of institutional research and in the context of analyses of the propagandistic elements of media (2002). She notes, for example, that British media theorists have placed what she considers undue emphasis on citizenship and agency in debates on childhood media. She recognises that British media theory does so in part to distance itself from the psychologistic model of media research in the United States, but she suggests that U.S. scholarship in fact employs a broad range of interdisciplinary models from which to observe media for children. What confuses the British, she suggests, is that the United States *does* have serious social problems and that there *are* heavy levels of media use in the context of an extraordinarily media-saturated cultural economy. U.S. children are indeed trained as citizens, but always as already mediated citizens.

To transfer these discussions to a Chinese context is rather difficult. Ideas of citizenship are internationally founded on very different political structures and thereby involve varying expectations of rights and responsibilities. Citizens embody widely differentiated levels of nationalistic, cultural, or ethnic intensity. This is also only the start of what might be an extensive discussion of the degree to which models of citizenship are also built on nation (birthright), cultural competency, and assumptions of social belongingness. Here I would simply argue that children's media assume Chineseness in terms of language, but also in political and cultural competency. The vanishing point for the citizenship values of children's film is that the quality of Chineseness is located in the geopolitical boundaries of the PRC, that it is normative and indeed preferable to other conditions. Films for children in China assume that their subjects and audiences are of a limited range of recognised ethnicities (the Han majority unless the film is specifically dealing with a particular minority group). "Other" ethnicities are always presented to give either a message of national cohesion or an internationalist edge to the film for prospective foreign sales. In *Cheer Up and Smile* (*Yangqi nide xiaolian* 2001), two children meet at a summer camp. One is a Chinese-American girl living with her mother, the other is a Chinese boy living with his father. They eventually discover that their parents were separated in the United States ten years earlier and that they are both Chinese, and brother and sister. The film tries at one level to address the issue of overseas Chinese with new national identities, but in the end cannot resist pulling the Americans back to China, where they "belong." The role of education and national curriculum materials (usually delivered through textbooks but also now through electronic media) is crucial in the transmission of cultural values and competencies. The contributors to Hein and Selden's (2000) collection of essays on historical memory in relation to the 1939–1945 wars and the U.S. war in Vietnam make a case for citizenship as conditional on the acceptance of certain local truths, "officially selected, organized, and transmitted knowledge" (Soysal 2000, 130). They argue that textbooks offer the prevailing official version of the nation's behaviour and responsibilities, although these may be strongly contested in the classroom by some teachers and outside the classroom by progressive or revisionist sections of society. Through textbooks first of all, children's media incorporate the explicit transmission of cultural value, versions of history, and political norms. The claim underlying history textbooks and the critique of these books is that competency in the classroom is central to the socialisation of children into the habits and expectations of a local understanding of social belongingness, which may or not be characterised at a political level as citizenship.

In the following chapter, the Film Course is discussed as an example of planned media literacy. It is not necessarily the case, however, that all media competencies contribute in the same way as classroom competency to a sense of citizenship through national cohesion. Certainly, *Little Sisters* and *Baseball Boy* are consonant with the direction of the nation at different points in time. The first film ties together morality, courage, ethnicity, the national project of modernization, and Maoist iconography. The second discusses national success as a partner to capitalist development. The latter film is seen, however, in a much more varied media context than the first. This is partly due to the obvious growth of internationalised television content for children (especially in animation) but is also due to a broader school curriculum. Textbooks published in 1997 for the science and technology curricula cannot discuss the perils of overpopulation and worldwide food shortages without referring to the interdependence of humanity worldwide. In a chapter discussing CFCs and the depletion of the ozone layer, a cartoon depicts a sixteenth-century court with three convicted criminals with the familiar boards slung around their necks announcing their crimes. Each criminal is a polluting factory, and the crime is murder. The image is intensely local, with rather unpleasant connotations of televised trials of corruption cases and drug dealing, and memories of mock trials in the Cultural Revolution where the accused may end up with a placard around their necks as they are condemned to execution. Yet the image also conjures up popularised notions of sixteenth-century law enforcement, and even non-Chinese readers might recognise the image of Judge Bao in the figure of the presiding official.

This image is a work of political socialisation—because it draws on stories of magistrates in the Ming era but also on contemporary memories of the rule of law. Children are presumed to recognise both sets of references. It is also a serious and internationally knowledgeable primary textbook on the effect of industrialization both in China and in the developed West. If the presence of Mickey Mouse and Pikachu complicate the media field for children outside school, so such textbooks make complex the idea of political socialisation through the media. This is an observation that has already been made in the Western domain, where one person's political socialisation is another's indoctrination. Whereas Australian researchers complain that there has been little work done on political socialisation because Australia is politically apathetic (Waniganayake and Donegan 1999), key names in the United Kingdom have dismissed the socialisation approach as inherently biased towards existing dominant models of politics themselves (Buckingham 1999). This argument is useful for the Chinese comparison in that it reminds the non-PRC researcher that, although the socialisation practices in China seem explicitly and undeniably political *and* ideological, there are nonetheless implicit strands of socialisation working throughout most media products for children across the world.

A project carried out in Western Australia in 2000 revealed that first generation Chinese migrants felt that Australian media were indeed not ideological enough——that they contained neither history nor culture——and were therefore failing as educational products (Donald 2001; Donald and Richardson 2003). However, an analysis of the (pre-school) programming thus dismissed suggested that the ideological content was embedded deeply into the programming—at a level visible only to those with a certain configuration of Australian cultural competency. The most effective ideological indoctrination may be the most insidious, the least visible. The power of ideological bias lies perhaps in its focus on those citizens contained and maintained as central to its everyday socio-political logic.

In Mainland Chinese debates, the issue of socialisation is important to social science and to an emerging culture of media study (Feng 2002; Zhang and Harwood 2002). There is a preferred model of behaviour acknowledged in these studies, one that media might support or undermine. The dominant model of politics is in evidence, very much so, and is not questioned in the literature. Whereas a radical edge in the U.K. and Australian research wants to see free-floating agency in the approach to child respondents and groups, and attaches political possibilities to that agency, even the more forgiving research in Chinese sociology (such as that practised at the Research Institute into Children and Teenagers) documents the pragmatics of modern youth without commenting on the political disintegration that might accompany such social flexibility.

There is, therefore, an apparent disagreement between international perspectives on the term "socialisation." Effects researchers tend towards a norm, which media act upon to produce divergence. Discussions in psychology and audience studies on the effects of media on children are numerous and well reported in the mainstream press in the United Kingdom, United States, and Australasia. Media harm is a recurring theme in much research into the content and "reality factor" of video games, television, and film. News stories reporting acts of violence by minors invariably routinely and cannibalistically seek out accounts of inappropriate media use as a contextual explanation of abhorrent behaviours in the young. Television foundations, non-government organizations, and film education societies are frequently set up to counter the perceived dangers of excessive advertising, and of animated and live action violence and sex on screen. These initiatives are impossible to qualify en bloc. Some are organised through particular religious ideologies, others are secular but based on a commitment to local product and sensibilities. Still others make creative challenges to industry on its own terms, producing countervailing product for competitive sale and distribution. In this last respect, the China Children's Film Studio (established 1981) and the Australian Children's Television Foundation (established 1977) have similar ideals at their core.

These research tendencies are connected to the ways in which societies demonstrate the collective relationship between adult and child. The nervousness with which many adults view their main methods of communication (at least when children enter the ecology of the audience) indicts the moral confidence of the social collective as much as it points to individuated schisms in taste, value systems, class expectations, fantasies of control, and patterns of responsibility and care.

As I argued in chapter 2, The Children's Film Studio is an instance of an incomplete institutional answer to a problem arising from a mismatch between competency, fantasy, and morality. The children of the reform era (*gaige*) were unreasonably expected to reform their competencies as children of a *new*, new China without at the same time needing new stories and new fantasy structures to accommodate their experience, and without alteration to the moral framework in their lives. In practice, the staff of the Studio found that they had to at least try to take on new ways of talking to children, and accept alteration in fantasies of contemporary childhood.

Television programming has taken on an international aspect for the same reason—the need to address children in ways that work for the audience, and is most successful when it blends stories that are recognisably Chinese, whilst allowing new modes of narration and unexpected fantasies to inhabit an old tale. The long-running remake of *Journey to the West* (*Xi you ji*, CCTV, 1999–2000) ran for fifty-two episodes of twenty-two minutes each. It was international standard in design, colour (stock), and sound. The film took an old classic, Monkey, Piggy, Sandy, and the monk Tripitaka's journey to the Buddha, and made it available to a young audience in the main by force of quality. It competed with foreign animation, but also offered landscapes that drew on traditional painting styles, characters that were already household names, and a series structure that—although the longest series animation ever made in China—fitted in with the generically extended soap series screened for adults. Merchandising was produced, five- and fifteen- centimeter-high rubber figurines of the main characters, cartoon books, and VCD copies were available after broadcast (but not before), and—most crucially for the show's critical longevity—university students saw it as a satire on power in the PRC.

The mediated entertainment of children may rely on moral injuncture, simple stories, educational methodology, and a desire for functional outcomes in terms of socialisation and competency. That understanding of media for children is arguably what fuelled much of the post-1949 production in China, where socialisation and politics were so closely bound into the competencies and qualities of a model citizen. This did not deny all agency to those generations, who were consuming competently *in context*. In the reform era, the situation is different. Children's negotiation of many available texts is more visibly a part of the new economy and of the tensions that challenge the state, the media industries, and the population.

NOTES

1. Established 1985 and awarded every two years. The Ministry of Film and Television (now SARFT) donated prize money from 1991.

2. International Children's Day was inaugurated at the 1925 Geneva Conference for the Protection of Children. Taiwan celebrates the day on 4 April; the United States around 12 October, whereas Japan combines the celebrations with other national celebrations in "Golden Week" (Donald 2002a, 211).

3. The exceptions will be children of first generation migrants running labour-intensive but capital-poor businesses to achieve the level of financial security required for successful settlement. It is likely, however, that these children will also receive as good an education as the parents can afford and will themselves prioritise education in their own families.

4. This expectation is enshrined in a somewhat cautious way in *The Convention on the Rights of the Child* (1993):

Article 32
1. States Parties recognize the right of the child to be protected from economic exploitation and from performing any work that is likely to be hazardous or to interfere with the child's education, or to be harmful to the child's health or physical, mental, spiritual, moral, or social development.
2. States Parties shall take legislative, administrative, social, and educational measures to ensure the implementation of the present article. To this end and having regard to the relevant provisions of other international instruments, States Parties shall in particular:
(a) Provide for a minimum age or minimum ages for admission to employment;
(b) Provide for appropriate regulation of the hours and conditions of employment;
(c) Provide for appropriate penalties or other sanctions to ensure the effective enforcement of the present article.
(UNESCO and the Convention on the Rights of the Child). Ironically, the United States had not ratified at time of promulgation.

5. Donald (and Chu), Small ARC-funded questionnaire, 1998: "How do you define childhood?" Thirty percent of respondents mentioned legal definitions to validate their response.

4

Classroom Media: Education and the Film Course

In a primary school in Jiangxi, grade 3 and grade 4 students (eight- to ten-year-olds) studied the story of Robinson Crusoe in several film versions over an entire semester. The aim of the course was to build a comprehensive understanding of survival and to build physical endurance amongst students. The teacher in charge argued that, although the catchment of the school was of low to average economic standing, many children in her year groups were single children, and many were somewhat spoilt as a result. She felt that visual appreciation, fun (happiness), and technological training could combine to support a moral agenda. She and her team utilised fieldwork in the surrounding countryside to help the children recreate the Robinson Crusoe story as a collective enterprise. They "survived" the field trips and made their own film to tell the story and comment on what they had learnt. The first scene in the children's film shows a seven year old coming home from school and collapsing in front of the television. As he stretches out on the sofa, his mother removes his shoes and brings him a snack. He does not utter a word of thanks nor offer to help her. This is the "Robinson Crusoe" (or little emperor) of Jiangxi, 2002!

The teacher told the story of the project to the conference delegates, and relayed the film through a power point using video and flash. The exercise combined the up-skilling associated with modernisation with the management of the self in a collective society that is an ongoing feature of moral education (jiaoyu) and socialisation in Chinese schools. It was facilitated by a demonstrably competent woman who manipulated technology in ways that accomplished comprehensive learning in a specific social environment according to state-approved and pragmatic moral standards of self-sufficiency, environmental awareness, and collective endeavour.

TEACHERS

In chapter 2 I argued that certain children's films since 1979 have evoked a thread of human feeling running between the experiences of the old and the expectations that cluster around the young. I suggested that, whilst this thread of *ganqing* evokes collective memories of revolutionary morality, this hypothetical thread also allows for some sort of secular continuity in an otherwise confusing moral and social environment. In this chapter the discussion addresses the link between education and childhood values as they are expressed and pursued in film in the classroom.

The role of media literacy has been cited as a progressive concept in children's media studies, and in education it is a good measure for new values in learning, teaching, and cultural behaviour. Its usefulness is partly that it describes a necessary aspect of both formal teaching, and of learning outside formal teaching. Media literacy can be tied to values that are conservative. It may also offer an effective counterattack on conservative value systems that undermine literacies, which seem to offer an alternative to print. In their play with the ideas and communicative techniques learnt from television, film, and comics, many children can be both expressive and competent but these ideas and techniques are not always valued as educational. How many children have been given credit for their encyclopaedic knowledge of Manga drawing styles, or of Sailor Moon's transformations, or of the dynamic cause and effect systems in Chuck Jones and Tex Avery's brilliant and globally devoured storytelling techniques? Not many. Even now, as the study of media in schools supports growing understanding of the value of multi-literacy (Silverblatt 1995; Cope and Kalantzis 2000), existing value systems privilege print and its own thread back to the cultural security of traditional and classical texts.

Teachers in the primary system in China have been the main source of the perspectives offered in this chapter and the gradual acceptance of media literacy was evident in conversations over a period of time. Interviews in 2000 and 2001 brought two themes strongly to the surface. First, teachers worried that children were losing a sense of historical perspective, and that this impacted on the teachers' ability to deliver the curriculum. There were too many irrelevant stories available to students, they felt, particularly through cartoons from Japan and the United States, which confused their understanding of central ideas of national priorities, models of behaviour, and China's past. Second, they felt that children needed to learn about new media technologies in order to be fully competent, but teachers felt themselves underprepared for the task. The problem fell first between the teachers' separation of technological skills and media content. The latter was again divided between the scope and challenge of media literacy and the actual content of children's preferred shows in a quasi-international market.

The uses of media in the Chinese education system are about quality: intellectual, physical, and moral development. Media literacy in this context has to be constantly qualified by culturally and politically differentiated understandings of the term. In China, literacy is connected to quality, which is itself connected to social attitudes and behaviour. The case studies here look at classroom media as a pedagogic requirement and at the Film Study program in primary schools. These studies address media research in terms of identity formation and collective socialisation, both of which are core goals in Chinese educational practice. The key concepts have been discussed in relation to film culture, and it is not a coincidence that they are also central to the education system. The first concept is education itself (that is, pedagogy and all-round education—*jiaoyu*), sociality (symbolic belongingness and control), competency (skills and confidence in a particular politico-cultural sphere), entertainment (structures of pleasure based on social norms), and fantasy (stories of fear and desire which underwrite social norms). These terms are in the main derived from children's media studies worldwide, and from film scholarship.

> Mass media are distinct from other potentially socializing institutions (schools, religious institutions) in several important ways: (a) Children's primary contact with them occurs informally as part of the home and family environment rather than in structured settings and activities; (b) with some important exceptions, the contents of mass media are not planned or designed to educate, to enhance development, or to socialize children into the mores of their culture. Instead media are often designed for entertainment or attracting audiences to advertisements; messages are conveyed but are incidental to the purposes of the producers; (c) children's exposure to mass media begins in infancy. Long before most children enter any formal educational setting, they have watched hundreds of hours of television, and some have also had extensive contact with books and other media. (Huston et al. 1994, 3)

This quote is taken from a collection edited by possibly the most respected psychologists working in the field of media and effects on children. Their considered remarks are useful for building a sense of how the starting points in the United States and in China are different, and therefore as a way of locating what is especially worth attention in describing China. Taking the points above one by one I would argue that point a is probably still true, although the early accession to kindergarten in more affluent urban areas suggests that organised activities will be a somewhat dominant feature of Chinese children's lives. Nevertheless, the penetration of TV and video/VCD into homes suggests that it is indeed the case that children will be receiving their first acculturation into visual media in domestic settings—or at least in the company of an extended family setting, perhaps in a private home or around a shared TV—but probably not in any setting more formal than that. Point c is probably accurate for most urban and many rural children. Television has a 97 percent penetration rate in China, and children will be watching it alongside adults. Poorer children will share smaller house-room with television and adults, whilst middle income children will be encouraged to watch English Disney from as early an age as possible to give them a head start in the race for educational advantage. They won't, therefore, all be using the television in the same ways, or to the same ends and competencies. Television penetration in China has led to a diversification of use rather than to a larger audience for mainstream programmes. The television may be "on" but it is as likely to be showing karaoke or a pirated VCD of *Purple Rain* (2001) or *Finding Nemo* (2003) as it is the CCTV children's schedule.

Point b is harder to tick off as a universal truth about media consumption. Media in China are in many instances specifically designed "to educate, to enhance development, or to socialize children into the mores of their culture." In the rubric of the China Children's Film Society (*Zhongguo ertong shaonian dianying xuehui*) it is stated explicitly that the society was founded (1984) in response to a CCP call (in 1981) "for the whole society to pay greater heed to the healthy development of children and adolescents, and train them as successors to the cause of Communism, generation after generation (*daidai xiangchuan*)."[1] The call came as a component of Party anxieties in the 1980s about the effects of marketisation on political loyalties, with a special meeting of the Central Committee convened 1 June 1981 to discuss how to maintain children's "mental health" through films, televisions, and picture books, "not through just schools."[2]

As I have discussed in relation to film production, the political and cultural socialisation of the young is a crucial factor in developing a succession to Chinese national integrity, social cohesion, and to ensure the long-term human potential of a strong developmental economy. It is not possible to separate education from sociality, which it maintains and reproduces. Sociality refers to the condition produced by the production, reproduction, and maintenance of a dominant form of being in society—often through education (Reuven and Rapoport 1990; Yogev and Shapira 1990). It is a somewhat broader concept than education in this application as it refers to the overall set of competencies and habits and behaviours, which a person learns to exhibit within a certain social setting. The key word in measuring sociality is the same word used above to suggest the disposition to agency, *competence*. Agency can indeed only happen in a condition of sociality, as both are based on competencies, which exclude as well as create the belongingness that promotes national identity, achieved citizenship, and culture. As discussed in the previous chapter on children's representation in film, it is crucial for children to achieve competence in the sociality of their place of residence, their homes, and their cultures. Without competency they are deemed and deem themselves anti-social and unhappy.

Competence may occur through socialisation with other children in the company of adults, or through the processes of mimetic development, which allow children to develop behaviours that mimic adult functions at the level of play, or through formal education, and they may also be acquired through interaction with media. Sociality may be nationally, internationally, or very locally specific, and occurs at many levels in a child's experience. Mediated socialization is clearly an enormously important part of modern childhood experience.

American cultural critic of childhood Henry A. Giroux has argued that:

> media culture . . . has become a substantial, if not the primary, educational force in regulating the meanings, values, and tastes that set the norms that offer up and legitimate particular subject positions—what it means to claim an identity as a male, female, white, black, citizen, noncitizen. The media culture defines childhood, the national past, beauty, truth and social agency. The impact of new electronic technologies as teaching machines can be seen in some rather astounding statistics. It is estimated that the "average American spends more than four hours a day watching television. 4 hours a day, 28 hours a week, 1,456 hours a year. (1999, 2–3)

It is the fact of media importance in modern socialisation that produces not just a strong centralisation of social experience, but also that causes anxiety, mistrust, and outright fear in the relationship between adults and media— even media which they themselves sanction as a social group, consume, and in which they participate as economic supporters, workers, and creative agents. This perhaps explains the ongoing attraction of effects research, and why *effects* are still more studied (and constructed) than the *competencies* produced by media use and familiarisation.

There is also a deep concern with media's facility at socialisation; in Western economies, these concerns focus on the ways in which corporate interests can and have become central to ideological structures of control in society. Disney (one of ten media conglomerates that have annual sales between ten billion and twenty-seven billion dollars) is one of a very few large corporations that hold the distribution rights to content and which also own the means of distribution—the television channels, the pay-tv deals, the videos, the English learning licenses, and the character licenses for associated merchandising and retail outlets. The fear in Chinese schools is that children will identify with the characters to which they have easy access— and thus identify with the entire Disney world of consumption and American family values. In more recent productions this has extended to a fear that the political advances of intercultural communications can be furthered and also appropriated by Disney versioning of the Other—the native American Indian, the Chinese heroine, the Mayan Indian, and so on. Susan Willis describes Disney as an "immense nostalgia machine," or, as Giroux puts it,

Disney's power lies in tapping into "lost hopes, abortive dreams, and utopian potential of popular culture" (1999, 5).

Similarly, research in Chinese society suggests that exposure to Western style advertising and media promotes aspirations towards consumer-led values. The tendency in cities "new" to consumerism is strongest amongst the young (Wei and Pan 1999). There are, for instance, concerns amongst teachers, government, and media workers that pornography is infiltrating the domestic sphere through television (Interviews, Beijing, 2000–2001). They cite the inappropriately elongated bodies of Japanese action heroines (*Sailor Moon*) as unduly "adult" in aspect and form. Local product does not compete adequately to ward off this apparent danger. Media professionals are also concerned that Chinese film and television workers are not communicating with children in sufficiently amusing and relevant ways to hold their attention and retain a share of the market. The metonymic "Disney" worry amongst Western researchers and commentators is also about the concentration of ownership, the return of vertical integration of product and distribution, and a paucity of variety and local, cultural responsiveness. However, the problem for Disney critics is that the films are *too* successful, *too* overweeningly seductive (but not at all obviously pornographic) for young minds, and *too* effective in their ideological pursuit of a particular fluffy pink but also red, white, and blue American dream. Chinese products are failing, they are too "pretty" for teenagers, and not sufficiently entertaining for younger groups, and are therefore losing out to the moral wasteland of foreign content.

Political socialisation is not a term much used by the contemporary Western researchers, but that is also an issue at play in their discussions. It is certainly an issue in Asian-based studies of children's media (especially Internet) use (Guntarto 2001; Komolsevin 2002). Socialisation is not a problematic idea in China, but the articulation of the competencies that it prefers certainly are; they make its workings as an ideologisation of the self quite apparent. Competencies are socially implicit signs of belonging, rather than measurable learnt behaviours. As an ex-lecturer, and current postgraduate student of the Chinese education system has said in conversation, "it all seems to be about whether our hair is properly bobbed rather than about any real morality. It is all about 'moral' behaviour, not about ethical judgement." Returning to interviews with teachers who are disturbed by Japanese "pornography," one can argue that the fear of pornography relates to a desire to define and hence control social competency in the management of the body, the boundaries of personal ethics, and the flows of familial and media interaction in the home, all of which are part of a teacher's sense of the role of education, and a measure of her competency in that system.

Japanese animation is ubiquitous on children's television and in the market in China, and combined with Disney, the international products make a most visible attack on the education system's control of the child's body. Disney educational VCDs and CD-ROMs are available in the big bookstores, supported by street market merchandising (a great deal of Disney merchandise is "Made in China"), by dubbed Disney cartoons on television, and by VCDs on street corners. Upmarket and very downmarket clothing stores feature Disney motifs alongside *Hello Kitty* and *Totoro* rip-offs, and the domestic *Lanmao* (*Blue Cat*) product. Urban children typically attend primary school with a Young Pioneer red scarf around their neck, a Mickey Mouse pack on their back, and a Pokémon or Nemo tag hanging from their belt buckle. The school curriculum forbids the use of Disney CDs in class, but well-off children have them at home instead. Disney thus sets up an alternative model for learning as fast-paced entertainment, whilst taking over the disciplined children's bodies of the educational system and delivering a hybrid to school in the morning. If citizenship is about shared cultural memories (of war, revolution, and struggle), shared values (family, collective responsibility, education), and mutual survival, then it is also about the ways in which those signifiers of belonging are worn on the body. In the opening scenes of *Lin Family Shop* (1959) a teenage daughter berates her merchant father (Xie Tian) for allowing her to wear imported Japanese clothes to school. The year is 1919 and Chinese youth are protesting Japanese gains in Manchuria. In 2002, primary teachers teach Japanese aggression and U.S. imperialism as core elements of modern Chinese history, but their pupils are wearing Japanese and American motifs with a casual disregard of capital's contradictions.

EDUCATION AND FANTASY

The sociologist of education Basil Bernstein once pointed out that pedagogy has to be "meant" if it is to be counted under the rubric of education. "It is necessary to distinguish between pedagogic consequences and a pedagogic relation. All experiencing carries a pedagogic potential, but all experiences are not pedagogically generated" (Bernstein 2000, 199). In children's media this is an important distinction in the main because it is very hard to separate intentions absolutely. A Disney or Hollywood family film is first and foremost entertaining; there are complex plot lines, good and consistent character development, aids to pleasure (music, colour, drama), and an overall familiarity in presentation that allows the viewer to relax and enjoy the show. The quote above on Disney as the "nostalgia machine" is pertinent here—for nostalgia is as much about the present as it is about the past. It is about loss, but also about wish fulfillment. It is the nub of attraction between fantasy and the social. Even, perhaps especially, fantasy is based on competency. It facilitates agency insofar as it gives form to experience, and allows both creator and consumer to tell stories about themselves.

The source and direction of fantasy in Chinese media for children is, however, in question. Behind the weakening of film culture, the internationalisation of television, the immaturity of the content in Internet and new media is a socially located dispute over whose fantasies should be served, whose creativity can best catch the mood of the contemporary Chinese child, and to what political end those fantasies should tend. The exaggerated worries of teachers when they look at the "pornographically" elongated bodies of Japanese *manga* may actually betray not just a sense that they are losing control of children's bodies, but also of the fantasies that structure their overall approach to the world.

They may not have cause for concern. Talking to children over four years it appeared that children themselves chose widely across Chinese and foreign content, and often assumed foreign content to be Chinese. Many attributed their choices to values that would support norms of patriotic socialisation. In a set of Year Four (nine- to ten-year-olds) interviews in 2002 we found that Harry Potter was "good" because he stuck up for his friends and was a hero. Hermione was liked because she is clever. There is nothing very radical here. However the poor but spirited red-haired larrikin Ron Weasley was not cited. One wonders why he did not slip into the favourite category of the brave but naughty boy. Perhaps that would have been too blatant and local a slip between a particular Chinese type, the *wantong*, and an international story.

The fantasy and sociality of these audiences is by definition entwined. Like much in the reform era it is contradictory. Teachers want media-skilled children, but don't want them to use the media! Parents are similarly confused. Television comes off badly relative to its obvious popularity—many children related that their Chinese parents felt television to be a waste of time—and child respondents suggested that they liked TV but knew that it was "just entertainment." Computers, feted in the 1980s as the ultimate symbol of technology, were much more widely approved, and institutionally are now the symbol of a modern educational environment. Parental suspicion of television has been described in the U.K. context as a "peculiarly English response to the relations between television, domesticity, and the suburban" (Oswell 2002, 98). In the 1950s, television "threatened" a version of an ordered hard-working nation, as much as it supported it in times of nation-building; the Coronation broadcast in 1953 is the oft-cited example (Oswell 2002, 99). A very similar debate is however evident in Chinese opinion, where television is both essential to nation-building, as Sun argues in her work on the Olympics (Sun 2002, 183–208), but where state subsidy for film and parental disquiet about "too much" television runs alongside the expanding possibilities of children's viewing habits. The functionality of television is invested in the symbolic work that it can do—and building the national morale through sports coverage is an obvious exemplar of this. It is harder to argue for Japanese- and U.S.-originated cartoons as important to children's symbolic accession to media use-as-literacy, advertising exposure, and pro-social understanding. Watching television is rather like doing politics, but without the teacher there to guide your response.

COMPETENCIES AND RIGHTS

Article 17 (The Convention on the Rights of the Child, 1993):

> States Parties recognize the important function performed by the mass media and shall ensure that the child has access to information and material from a diversity of national and international sources, especially those aimed at the promotion of his or her social, spiritual and moral well-being and physical and mental health. To this end, States Parties shall:
>
> (a) Encourage the mass media to disseminate information and material of social and cultural benefit to the child and in accordance with the spirit of article 29;
>
> (b) Encourage international co-operation in the production, exchange and dissemination of such information and material from a diversity of cultural, national and international sources;
>
> (c) Encourage the production and dissemination of children's books;
>
> (d) Encourage the mass media to have particular regard to the linguistic needs of the child who belongs to a minority group or who is indigenous;
>
> (e) Encourage the development of appropriate guidelines for the protection of the child from information and material injurious to his or her well-being, bearing in mind the provisions of articles 13 and 18.

If the thread of *ganqing* stubbornly ties together film content and the political memories of the older generation in China's children's film elites, it also works in the pursuit of educational goals and the embrace of new media in the classroom. In the politically inspired work of Mab Huang there is another thread, the appeal to history in "the red thread" of liberalism, an enduring and continuing link to emerging models of human rights values in China, and one which excuses change in favour of continuity. Gloria Davies has also argued that there is a red thread linking the old with the new, as Chinese intellectuals work with a belief in the social power of intellectual endeavour, whilst fashioning new paradigms of engagement with Chinese and Western theoretical trajectories (Davies 2001, 4 and passim). The unfashionable and often unmarketable products of the studio system are also in some kind of conversation with new times, an "in-public" engagement across cultural production and social experience. Li Honghe (cf. chapter 2) made *I Am a Fish* simply because he needed a job, and to expand his experience as a feature director, and he knows that he may never make another children's film.[3] But the making of the film taught him something about integrity and courage in the face of official misunderstanding. He stood up for his film and in the process stood up for the integrity of the child audience.

These threads may be arbitrary metaphors for quite different desires, but they do share an ethical concern with keeping alignment between the past and the present. The connectivity across generations, across political aspirations, and across intellectual projects of the past century is an approach to belongingness in a rapidly developing society. The "thread" for media competencies is very much that of *jiaoyu*, horizontal and vertical education in skills, information, culture, and history. *Jiaoyu* encompasses school-based learning, Young Pioneer and Youth League activities, and overall socialisation, but also the "education" of children in the family (*jiaowai jiaoyu*), from playing the piano, to housework, to swimming.[4]

The subject of education needs, therefore, always needs explanation in an English language publication. Education is translated as *jiaoyu* and vice versa. It is not however a very precise translation, as education in China includes a great deal of cultural and historical weight that might not be included in the English use of the word. To illustrate this, I will give an extended summary of the research carried out in Australia in parallel to work in China in 1998. The subject was film memory of first generation Chinese migrants. What emerged was a subtle differentiation between television-based education for children in Australia and *jiaoyu*.

The finding that informs the discussion here is that many parents prioritised history (*lishi*) and education (*jiaoyu*) in their descriptions of appropriate media culture. The term cropped up in discussions and on questionnaires as a way of delineating the difference between what was Australian and what was Chinese. History was set up as "different" from entertainment, and from skills-based educational material, such as is found on, say, *Sesame Street*. Embedded cultural content in U.S. or Australian shows was not recognised as such (*wenhua*), mainly because of the apparent absence of history. Parallel research, carried out in Beijing in the same year, produced statements about the nation (*guojia*), and culture (*wenhua*), but history was not mentioned as a pillar of cultural meaning, except where teachers complained that children could not understand revolutionary history very well. This suggests that history is, broadly speaking, a given in a national context, but may be missed in a diasporic situation. The distinction between history and memory may be muddied where particular historical narratives form part of cultural memory at distance.

When the interviewer brought *lishi* specifically into the conversation in Beijing, respondents acknowledged its importance to national sensibilities, and the difficulties of keeping the younger generation informed. There was not, however, the sense of urgency that was articulated in the work in Australia. It seems that, once the homeland has been left behind, the valorisation of historical knowledge emerges as a crucial indicator of nostalgic trauma for

China Best! Line drawing by child respondent, 2002.

VCD cover: Little Soldier Zhangga. *Courtesy Blue Cat Productions.*

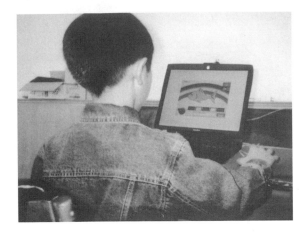

Useability testing of "English" CD-ROM (2001), author photograph.

Little Wooden Head *(Director: Xie Tian).*

The Film Fox! Zibo International Children's Film Festival Logo, 2002, designed for Shandong combining literary giant Pu Songling's fox fairy with child-oriented cartoon.

VCD covers: Sanmao's Travels *(top),* Sanmao Joins the Army *(bottom).*
Courtesy Blue Cat Productions.

Baseball Boy *(2002). International Film Catalogue, Zibo.*

Child's painting (1970s). Worker Teacher Takes Us to Collect Radishes.

Shopping centre, Children's Day, 2000, author photograph.

Murderers. *"Twenty-first century" science textbook, Guanxi.*

"Being Little Red Chicken." Classroom "film" exercise, 2002.

Classroom scene, Beijing 2001.

Teaching English, Beijing, 2001, author photograph.

"Manga-style" English textbook (Tsinghua University Press).

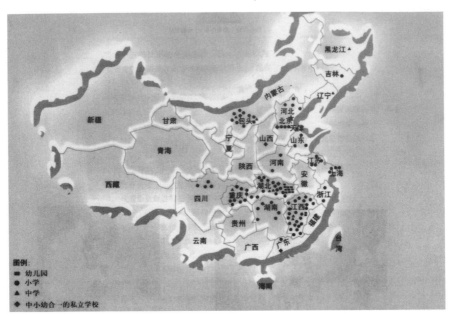

Test schools for the Film Course.

Storyboard: Lotus Lantern.

parents. It is also feasible to argue that, given the strength of Chinese nationalism in the PRC and amongst migrants from the PRC, that first generation overseas Chinese feel unable to articulate loss through the word "nation (country-*home*)" (*guo*jia), and must resort to the less poignant term, "history" (*lishi*). Perhaps too, as the research in Beijing suggested, *lishi* means both immediate revolutionary history and the longer histories of the Chinese people, whereas *guojia* carries stronger connotations of the nation and home as one and the same place.

In a telling exchange during one discussion, a partial exception is made for the Disney film *Mulan* (1998) (these parents saw the Western version with their children in local cinemas and on video—not the Chinese version redubbed for the Chinese market):

> *female 1*: Yes, the characterisation is good, the story is good, the subject theme is good, it has educational value, and the way of expression is good, the music is good and the colours are good.
> (general agreement)
> *male 1:* I think cartoon films are important in directing children's morality. I think that the most important thing in educating children is to educate their morality, children need to be educated on morality from a very young age.
> *male 2:* Yes, that is Chinese, but western programmes are, basically, almost, have no moral educational values. At least they are very rare.

In talking about media education, and educational value in Chinese media, it is therefore important to differentiate culturally saturated *jiaoyu* from "early learning." This opposition is rather different from the education versus entertainment dichotomy posed by Western critics of children's TV, although in some ways it supports the advocates of (especially pre-school) programming, which claims that it achieves education *through* entertainment. It would be profoundly disturbing to the Western programmers to discover that Australian-Chinese fathers opposed the entertainment and educational values of Australian children's television to the very concept of culture: "here, films tend to use local things, cats and dogs to make a narrative, they don't produce films from the perspective of cultural background" (male 3). Clearly the skills-based competencies of pre-schoolers' television were either not visible to this respondent, or they were dismissed because they were not embedded in a cultural competency that he could value.

The use of local media emerged as a competency with ambivalent value in the migrant situation, partly because the competency belonged to the child, not the adult, and therefore the adult could not necessarily see it as educationally worthwhile. Education is a concept that spans the global spectrum of rights. Children deserve either equality in opportunities, or equivalence, depending on the level of economic pragmatism of the speaker, and the degree of gender bias. In China, the high value of education is hard to overestimate, but its application countrywide is less certain. Despite the edict on nine years of *compulsory* schooling (1995), the actual levels of attendance depend on gender, parental income, place of residence, and, in agricultural areas, the time of year. Moreover, since the return of the exam and credential system in the reform era, urban and elite children are statistically as well as anecdotally privileged (Tang and Parish 2000, 65). Rural absences (Khan and Riskin 2001, 87–88) are a cause of constant concern to the Chinese government and to education officials, who are working on the finessing of new curricula to suit new times, whilst also working on rural support schemes to get more children in school. Unlike some other aspects of international human rights discourse, the rights of the child are not disputed in China, but they are not always deliverable.

The education and rights thread also ties children into the discourse of what has been nominated Asian values, and of more long-serving Chinese value systems,[5] in which core principles of humanism (*ren*), righteousness (*yi*), propriety (*li*), wisdom (*zhi*), and trust (*xin*) are ideally played out through stable family relationships and hierarchies, in harmony and conformity through social relationships generally, and with an expectation of morality in social-political organization. As such, it is notable that the seemingly retrogressive, or at least antimarket, element of moral socialisation in children's media in the PRC context, is quite contemporary in respect of values and political agendas in other predominantly Chinese societies (especially Singapore).

The (so-called) Asian Values system has been generally associated with the political cynicism of the southeast Asian region, with China as a late-comer-copycat of an alternative model of capitalist morality as defined elsewhere in Asia (Rodan 1996; Mab Huang 2000). Recent articles have argued that China (*zhongguo*) does not see itself as Asian (*yazhou*) (Korhonen 2002; Baik 2002), except insofar as the discourse of Asian values invites broad social compliance and is therefore economically productive. Nevertheless, some of the morally fundamental components of Confucianism also seem to be at play in the attitudes of older film-makers and studio workers, and are evident too in the attitudes of educationalists. Their cluster of values— embedded in stories of old men and their grandchildren—speak to *ren*, *yi*, *li*, and *de*. This cluster does not, however, have the power to mobilise economies and populations in the way the Asian Values discourse has been activated to support regional development. As Mab argues, the discourse is there but its contradictions are quite apparent. Tradition is an excuse for avoiding the duties of intellectual freedom, whilst pretending to a regionally located account of modernisation:

> Many papers on Confucian ethics tend to be nostalgic. They tend to succumb to the hope that the honorable traditions could somehow be adapted to the needs of our time . . . [the] attack on Confucian values and traditional political struc-

ture as well as family system [is] a red thread that [runs] through Chinese liberalism up to our time. (Mab 2000, 228)

Likewise, the appeal to moral and model-based education as a foundation for children's political socialisation also seeks to defuse the choices and negotiated contradictions inherent in the mediated reality that they occupy. Belongingness continues to be at the core of education and media, but the nature of the belonging is insecure, and so jealously guarded. The stories of collective virtue so much in evidence in animation and early films of the 1980s are now siphoned through a generational nexus of intrapersonal, intergenerational responsibility and care. This does not contradict, but it does offer a perspective on, Mab's demand for an internationalised version of human rights "the end of every political institution is the natural and imprescriptable rights of man" (Mab 2000, 232), and Blecher's sympathetic account of the downgrading of the collective ethos: "the sense of belonging to some larger whole—a community, a work unit, a class struggling against its exploiters, a socialist project, even a nation—that had begun to develop in the Maoist period, albeit in very problematic ways, is practically gone" (Blecher 1997, 212).

Marc Blecher's point is well taken. The advent of socialist capitalism has not developed strong categories of belongingness, nor has it produced a move towards a civil-society/liberal-democracy paradigm of autonomous association. As leading historians and political scientists attest year upon year, civil society is not in any case the best frame in which to look for public activity in the People's Republic.[6] China is neither socialist nor capitalist, neither centrist nor local, neither collective nor individuated. Its socialist market depends on all of these things at once. This is clearly a problem if the population fractures in response to the contradictions inherent in the changed economic model. Whereas some have done very well from marketisation, others are less fortunate. The dangers of "jumping in" (*xia hai*) with the market economy will not be lost on workers made redundant (*xiagang*) in the wake of retrenchments at the more unwieldy state-owned enterprises,[7] nor on peasants whose incomes have not kept pace with the costs of modernisation. If, at the same time, there are failures of government transparency at provincial levels, whilst nationally sponsored campaigns extol the three successes of 2001–2002 (the Olympic bid, the WTO accession, and qualifying for the World Cup Soccer finals), it is easy to see that a sense of disillusionment is a probable response from many Chinese citizens. Flemming Christiansen makes the point that the political economy of China in the reform era has focused on "nurturing the development of *public choice*, [but at the same time] has encompassed state intervention and regulation aimed at *manipulating public choice*" (2002, 177). The logical dynamic behind this focus—that people will choose economic development as it is in their own self-interest to do so—does not deal with the large numbers who cannot choose at all. Embedded in these mixed prospects are 350 million children, some of whom will take benefit from educational opportunities and prosper with China. Others will miss out and end up "cheap rather than skilled" (Christiansen, 188).

Children's role in the future of China is imagined and promulgated at the highest levels of political thinking, but these are activated in the main through educational initiatives. In the wake of twenty years of a one-child policy, the priceless wonder of a single child is self-evident and even pragmatic.[8] The rising cost of a good education is more manageable for one child than for many, and, if that child is an affluent urban girl, she is very lucky that this is now the case. Student choice of school is an issue for the Ministry of Education, with students and parents applying for enrollment in schools with good exam results and extracurricular offerings. The scarcity of children also induces parents to worry excessively about their achievements. News stories tell horrific tales of child suicides induced by the pressure of homework. The following news excerpts paint a solemn portrait of youth, pressure, and, particularly, of parents from outlying provinces pushing their children hard to make it out to the big universities. It is also apparent that, even though the system is attempting to reduce the demands on children's time, parents take up the "slack" with additional out-of-school study. This is not "out-of-school" (*jiaowai*) socialisation as much as force-feeding international competencies on children whose school day already runs from 8:00 AM to 3:30 PM.

Tian Tian, a twelve-year-old girl in north China's Shanxi Province recently killed herself, leaving a letter behind. "Dear parents, I can hardly express my gratitude to you for bringing me up in the past twelve years," it read. "But, I feel under such pressure. There is too much homework for me. I had no choice but to die. Last words from your daughter."

Sun Yunxiao, deputy director of the China Youth and Children Research Center, said: "Though children nowadays enjoy a much better living and study environment than their parents, they are overwhelmed by a kind of invisible pressure and can hardly feel the pleasures of life."

Tian Tian's primary school worked out rules for lightening the study burden on pupils several years ago. On average, it takes a pupil an hour a day to finish his or her homework. Then why do so many students feel under such great pressure?

Qin Jinliang, a professor with the Education Department of the Shanxi Normal College, said: "The homework assigned by teachers obviously has been reduced in recent years. But, examinations of all sorts have become popular, exerting great pressure on students." Pupils are forced to attend amateur classes on painting, playing musical instruments, dancing, math, and calligraphy or accept tasks assigned by their parents on weekends. Over half the students in big cities have attended Olympic classes on math, physics, and chemistry because the courses give them a chance to be enrolled by key schools after graduation. Some pupils attend two or three courses after school. According to a sample survey in Nanjing, afterschool training courses take up 57 percent of children's spare time, while *children in some developed countries spend over 90 percent of their spare time on sport or whatever they like*. (author's italics)[9]

The final sentence in the report compares the laxity of adult demands in the developed world to the heavy learning load on children in China. Whilst the report may be quoting statistics from the European Union or UNESCO (it does not give a source) the figure of 90 percent has not been broken down by socioeconomic level, which would give it more purchase. What it does do is give a sense of popular opinion, and of a tension not unrelated to the ambivalence towards television discussed previously. The parental problematic might be stated as: Children are precious so we must make them happy, but our precious children are also scarce within the context of a single family, so we must also make sure that they succeed.

Children are (relatively) scarce only because adults are already so numerous; "relatively" as there were approximately 58 million children (under five years old), 350 million under 15, 380 million under 17, in China in 2002.[10] In 1953, children made up 37 percent of the population, by 1990 this proportion had fallen to 28 percent and, by 1997, to 25 percent.[11] Scarcity brings value, but it is a value that is meted out in accordance to location and to the rural-urban divide. As it is a relative scarcity rather than an numerical one, there is a great deal of political but also actual capital invested in childhood. The scale of this expenditure and the responsibility of the rights for so many young people should be recalled in China's favour, even though there are some contradictory and worrying tendencies also evident. Urban areas have a lower birth rate than do rural zones, but rural children suffer a higher death rate (5:7). However, given that it is suspected that unregistered births happen most in the countryside, the actual rate might be rather higher. The statistics show an unusual male to female gender differential in the 0–4 age group (118:100) that strongly indicates that selective abortion and neglect of girls are increasing.[12]

Gender inequality is an indicator of the different experiences of different child populations in the PRC (Greenhalgh 1993). Even before birth there is differential treatment, and this continues when girls are not prioritised in parental decisions on education, or when the State discriminates against them in graduate access to tertiary entrance (Shi 1995). Access and participation, the core principles of a dynamic media environment, are by no means constant in China, at home or at school.

The media focus on the absolute version of value of "childhood" has been strong for over twenty years, and has made attempts to combat gender bias.

Family planning campaigns used posters in the early 1980s to propound the happiness associated with one beloved child; the picture was often that of a daughter. In a poster advertisement for the latest national census, the illustration depicts four adults and one child in the family, three generations in an inverted pyramid.[13] Even prior to the reforms, the media metaphor of children as flowers was a feminine image of political succession and sociality. In the late 1990s, the image remained but the emphasis shifted somewhat back to the child as a flowering of domestically managed virtue. Jiang Zemin's pre-retirement call for the return of virtue (*de*) in social and political life is symptomatic of an ongoing engagement with a politics of sociality, one that depends on children as its lynchpin in the popular imagination.[14] It may also be a conscious engagement with the hierarchies of those same (now rather less fashionable) Singaporean-Asian values that suggest a recoiling from real change in a new economy. Virtue (*de*) is another Confucian concept and not one readily associated with Communist rule, its reintroduction into political keywords makes it a family affair, insofar as it relates social ills back to the responsibility of the home and school through the emotional "pricelessness" of their offspring.

Child rights and the media in China are subject to the rhetorical whims of the leadership, but they are also a staple of the social imaginary in which that leadership must operate. The focus on pre-Liberation child suffering as opposed to post-Liberation opportunity is a theme that cannot be swept away, and one that adds force to every policy effort to improve the lot of the underprivileged child in China. The reports of child deaths in school-based firework factories, of the abandonment of baby girls and the abduction of sons for remote communities are the horrific end of child abuse. But the chronic challenges are more mundane, the development of media literacy for a large and diverse population, the inclusion of the poor in a highly merchandised mediated polity, and the possibility of quality (*suzhi*) for those who cannot afford to belong.

CLASSROOM MEDIA

"The essence of education is to improve the quality of the citizen" (Gu Mingyuan 2001, 23),

> Education (*jiaoyu*) is the basis of the socialist modernization drive, and the State (*guojia*) ensures priority to the development of educational undertakings. The entire society should show concern for and give support to the development of educational undertakings. The entire society should respect teachers (*jiaoshi*). (Article 4, *Education Law of the People's Republic of China* 1995)

Classroom media can be divided into three key areas: technological skills building, media education, and media-assisted curricula subjects. The first focus has been evident in China since the reform era began. Computer literacy is a continuing focus in curriculum development and in the process of benchmarking school facilities against international ideals and domestic targets. Media education is an emerging area of study, and is explored below through a case study of the Film Education initiative 2000–2002. Media assistance in general curriculum teaching is developing alongside international developments in media access, and in China is targeted at English language competency. All of these facets of media technology in the classroom are part of an ongoing and substantial set of educational reforms. They also entail a growth in media literacy that will underpin the creative competencies of the present generations of children.

Education reform is symptomatic of the need to move away from the chaotic radicalism of the late 1960s and early 1970s (Pepper 1996, 381), and to modernise China's economy. The educational responses to economic change have been discussed in important studies and scholarly collections (Hayhoe 1992; Pepper 1996; Rosen 1992; 1995) and continue to be debated in the light of curriculum development and the intensification of the modernising process. The teachers themselves incorporate curriculum objectives, the challenges of literacy in an uneven educational environment, and the position of children in national development (Rosen 1992; 1995).

Educationalists now prioritise visual communications and communicative events in the Chinese classroom and, a related theme, multiliteracies for teachers and students (Anstey and Bull 2000; Garton 1997; Durrant and Green 2000). Visual communications is a broad concept, encompassing all media communications with a visual component, and has been usefully identified by the journal of the same name as "the use of visual languages and technologies in . . . multi-modal genres, texts and communicative events."[15] Communicative events range from the personal text message embroidered with smilies and scare quotes to the announcement of policy changes in *The People's Daily*. They are less often associated with the practice of education as embodied in teacher-student communications, but it is this everyday practice that can be identified as a chain of communicative events, fundamental to the formation of young people's engagement with the institutions of state and society. The classroom is the locus for the key communicative event in children's daily lives.

The importance of education to Confucian Chinese society is well documented (Zhu 1992). So too is the position of the teacher as a guide and mentor to the student. The *laoshi/jiaoshi* title enshrines both a descriptive title, "teacher," but also an expectation of moral integrity, and a sense of continuity in culture and social behaviours, a thread between knowledge, history, and cultural value. The assumption of this role by the usually female *teacher* is important as, in revolutionary culture more generally, leadership was a role generally ascribed to men. There were inspiring cinematic women too (and roles taken by the actresses Tian Hua and Yu Lan are the best examples), but they tended to look up to male counterparts and thereby model the modelling process for the audience. The model citizens held up as examples to adults and children were men and women, but it was the men (Chen 1968; Lei 1990), who benchmarked the moral order of a revolutionary society. The status of the teacher is also clear in films spanning the period 1949–1980, where children's or family films in particular concentrated far more on the idealised teacher than on the parent-child relationship.

The post-1949 teacher has been a figure of—generally female—power in the discourse of revolutionary and liberated China. S/he was (and arguably still is) in the vanguard of change through her work in political socialisation of the young (most dramatically articulated in the Little Red Schools of the Cultural Revolution period, but more consistently in the instatement of national curricula and the distribution of national textbooks). Prior to the modernisation efforts of reform, s/he carried some of the responsibility for producing an educated mass able to contribute to a partial modernisation of China, from a society based on privilege to one organised through national priorities and development plans. As Pepper argues, this responsibility was not achievable in the exam-based, urban-focused educational system of pre-1965 (Pepper 1996, 365 and passim). Nonetheless, she more or less successfully taught literacy and numeracy skills to many children, which would serve them and the nation whatever political (factional) group was in the ascendancy. When young people were encouraged to turn against bad class elements in the mid 1960s and reinvent continuing revolution, the attack on teachers was then both inevitable and tragic. They did indeed embody the communication of state policy to young people, and even though not all were engaged in political instruction and monitoring, nonetheless it was impossible to be a teacher without wearing the mantle of the state in the eyes of teenagers and younger children. This period was the nadir of teaching as a class position in modern China. Given that it also marked a depression in cultural activity, especially film-making, the coterminous rise of media education and education itself as national priorities is unsurprising.

Teacher quality (and skilled teacher shortages) were pressing problems in 1976 and are so today. These shortages threaten the requirements of classroom technologies: "Learn to know, learn to do and learn to develop themselves" and the implementation of the nine-year education policy, and the desire to create a "scientific and humanistic spirit" (Gu 2001) based on the all-round moral education of all children.

Twenty years of reform has produced a competitive, outcome-driven society, with a focus on the new. A commensurate shift in pedagogic thinking has also occurred, and changes to the curriculum and to teaching styles are underway. Whilst there is a strong demand for vocational "post-WTO" training,[16] many of the advocates of change advise a soft approach to teaching that emphasises technology but which also makes the knowledge canon more relevant to the interests of students. Proposals also criticise the difficulty of the 1990s curriculum, which, it is argued, has changed only slightly from the 1960s model, and which favours only the cleverest students (Gu 2001, 21–23). The most far-reaching proposal is to introduce comprehensive (practical, academic, and contextual learning) education in areas, which may appeal to the gifted students, but also to the larger majority of average ability learners. These subject areas include information technology, community services, social research, fieldwork, and general technology. Starting in 2001, elementary and secondary schools were strongly encouraged to initiate courses in IT, and to teach students using Internet technology. The aim was to get all schools networked by 2003 (Gu 2001, 22). Experimental schools were set up in the mid 1990s to accommodate these priorities, and their promotional literature looks mainly at teacher qualifications, "scientific management" (*kexue de guanli*), resources, and multimedia equipment.

The new technologies of teaching are most apparent in language learning. The curriculum reform requires language tuition to start younger than in previous years. Literature looks mainly at teacher qualifications, "scientific management" (*kexue de guanli*), resources, and multimedia equipment. In major cities (Beijing, Shanghai, Guangzhou), students start at Grade One. More usually, they begin in grade 3. To support these guidelines, new textbooks have been produced at Tsinghua University and trial-tested across twenty-two provinces. The textbooks were designed by a young illustrator, and written by a professor of education.[17] They emphasise interactive teaching, fun, and a contemporary style of illustration.

The aim of the books is to professionalise the teaching of English through carefully graduated modules, which will eventually stretch from grade 1 up to grade 9. The series also makes language-learning fun and meaningful for urban and rural students, by drawing on easily (TV) accessed contemporary youth culture to support the experience of "English" in the classroom. Therefore the design of the books is funky, *manga*/animé-themed and loosely aligned to the fairy tale world of Japanese cartoons on children's TV and Disney stories on commercial English-learning VCD series. The textbook programme feeds into a broader set of initiatives. Current proposals at the Ministry of Education level seek to establish bases in institutes of higher education to train masters of foreign language education.[18] The training culminates in an examination process and a one-year placement in schools.

Increasingly, teachers access the computers in language labs to prepare other teaching aids for other subjects: powerpoint presentations and flash files are especially helpful for classes of up to forty students. Increasingly too, and in accord with Ministry guidelines, large campuses at well-funded high schools and at the university level use the intranet for class teaching, and to assist students in the assignments. Online learning draws on teachers' tips, assignment details, and source materials, as well as discussion forums where students can seek extra help and exchange ideas on the subject topics. The extension of the teacher's modality through the use of, say, after-class communications, is a significant factor in the modernisation of the teacher's role in the PRC. There has long been an assertion of the teacher as both in-class figure of authority and out-of-class mentor and political-social guide. Now, the teacher's access to technology produces her as a skilled and technologised communicator, who is also charged with the "out-of-classroom" (*jiaowai jiaoyu*) care of the students.

ROBINSON CRUSOE AND *GULLIVER'S TRAVELS*

The current moves to develop coherent media education in schools draws on the soft technology and child-centred media skilling that characterises feminised technological competence. The results are exciting as they indicate the positive end of socialisation in an explicit political environment, but they are driven by centralised notions of educational need. In April 1987 the Ministry of Propaganda (Public Information) (*Zhonggong zhongyang xuanchuan bu*) and the Ministry of Broadcasting, Film, and Television (*Guangbo dianying dianshi bu*) (now SARFT), together with the National Teachers' Association, issued a joint discussion paper: "Perspectives on Strengthening the Development, Dissemination, and Clarification of Children's Film." That called for extensive commitments from children's fun palaces (*shaonian gong*), schools, cinemas, and youth activity centres to make film accessible to children. It was followed in 1996 by renewed calls from the Ministry of Culture and the Teacher's Association for more access but also for a deepening of children's understanding of visual media, film, and television, and for educationalists in particular to take up this challenge given the new foreign content that would enter the country after China's accession to the World Trade Organisation.

In 2002, an international conference on the Film Course Experiment for Chinese primary schools was held in Shandong province. The conference discussed this extensive pilot course as one of the responses to the 1996 call for action. The Film Course was set up by Wang Liuyi (from Blue Cat Television productions),[19] the China Children's Film Association, and the project team on students' film education at the National Audio-Visual Teaching Aid Centre under the auspices of the Ministry of Education in Beijing. The ambition of the project is to increase film literacy in the classroom across the country, with a strong emphasis on films as conveyors of international and historical information, and films as sources of pleasure in learning for young people. First implemented in 1995,[20] reviewed in a discussion paper in 1999, debated in *The People's Daily* (*renmin ribao*), and then the subject of teacher assessment in 2001–2002, the programme works from the following stated motivations:

1. To increase understanding of national differences worldwide, and thus enlarge students horizons;
2. To develop a "world outlook" in students;
3. To use film to provide comprehensive approaches to knowledge gathering and the national curriculum—i.e., *Around the World in Eighty Days* can be worked into course materials on "literature, geography, history, biology, art, music, and sports"; and
4. To promote happiness in the classroom, and to thereby develop visual sophistication in students.

In the first stage, over fifty primary schools (*xiao xue*) were involved. Each school received copies of five hundred films included in the project. Teachers then chose films to screen in ninety-minute or two-hour classes. Some schools used as few as 20 titles, some as many as 420, with an average over the tested schools of 92. As the case studies below indicate, schools that were selective and inventive with the films tended to get the most interesting results in terms of curriculum linkages. Children were encouraged to respond to the films on paper and in discussion, but no assessed work or exams were set for the course. Again, individual teachers worked against this in some respects as they soon discovered that just showing a child a film does not necessarily elicit visible outcomes, and so some exercises were introduced to give some structure to the classes. This was not the original point of the research but it was a foreseeable response from teachers used to managing large classes and working towards strict achievement benchmarks.

The plan was to conduct experiments for two years and then to extend the program via the mechanism of the national curriculum, and its emphasis on "comprehensive teaching." Comprehensive student "quality" is addressed in terms of course comprehension and skilling, but also in relation to the subjectivity of the student as "all round" media literate person. "All round" includes their vision of a wider world, which may be already quite accessible and familiar to middle class urban children but will not be so to children in rural schools. It also includes an expectation that happiness is predicated on learning in a conducive environment and that the latter is characterised by multi-literacy, both visual and moral, in the classroom. The motivations underlying this set of objectives flesh out what is meant by a technological classroom and a "comprehensive curriculum." The modernisation process is accompanied by education objectives that position the teacher as an embodiment of new technologies, and as a mediator of external realities in the wider world. They also still take on responsibility for incorporating the political boundaries of state and Party in their management of the information that they convey—through film and language subjects. The Film Course exceeded the notion of "enlarging student horizons"[21] by also enabling teachers to improve their own status as modern educators.

There is a rigid version of child psychology working in the research component of the Film Course project. Although flexibility and absence of assessment criteria are mooted as the main planks of the teaching mode, the background work is clearly geared at socialisation into a particular psychologised worldview of human nature. The chief psychologist for the Film Course project, Shi Jiannong (a man in his late thirties), gives the following anecdotal reasons for his interests in children and visual media:

> Either because of the sparseness of cultural life of the time when I was young, or because of the great influence of films on children, the films I saw twenty years ago left a great impression. It was very normal for my peers and I to walk several kilometers from one village to another to see a film. Several kilometers may not be far for an adult but it is a long way for an eight- or nine-year-old child. It is a challenge . . . even if he is strongly motivated. Because of the shortage of film copies at that time, reels of one film were shared amongst several villages and shown in the open air. In order to have a film shown in different villages at the same time, people had to send a copy from one village to another on foot. Children followed the film projectionists from village to village so they could enjoy the movies again. Sometimes we had to walk more than ten kilometers in an evening. It seems incredible today that children would walk several kilometres just to see a film again and again, but it was very common for children in remote villages in the 1970s. (Shi et al., trans. Li Ling 2002)[22]

Shi's research project, with Wang Liuyi and Lei Zhenxiao, is based on work he has done on the structure of human nature and on the Quality Education model, (EHBN—Education Based on Human Nature), which emphasises "human all-round quality" over the consumption of knowledge (the "*suzhi*" supported by educational authorities in the PRC). The schema is alarmingly straightforward:

> In our opinion, the EBHNM is an educational intervention based on human nature. The purpose is to cultivate and maintain the appropriate behaviours or traits of a human being.
>
> [The] human being has three features: a) he is a biological individual with physiological features, b) he is a mental individual with intellectual features, c) he is a social individual with social features. (Shi et al., trans. Li Ling 2002)

This version of the human being translates as we have seen into a tripartite educational structure focusing on physical, intellectual, and social education. Although a feminist, or indeed almost any extranormative approach to the structure of human nature might be rather unimpressed by this depoliticisation of the subject; nonetheless, Shi's ideas produce a famously empty mould in which to place almost any ideological clay. The research model continues to extrapolate the main aims of the three parts of education:

Physical education: Eugenics, Genetics, Nutrition, Medical Care, Exercise, Sport
Psychological education: Cognition, Emotional development, Cultivation of a good personality, Perseverance
Socialization education: Self-consciousness, Social morality, Knowledge of the Law, Sense of social responsibility.

These are the aims and objectives of school and home-based learning. They are, Shi, Wang and Lei report, especially difficult to attain because of the growth of the one-child family. Film is part of the answer and they claim that their Film Course experiment proves it.

. . . [M]ovies affect not only children's socialization, but also increase their knowledge, values . . . , independence, perseverance and interest in physical exercise. (4)

They base these claims on questionnaires administered to eight hundred grade 2 to grade 5 students, half from the Film Course contingent and half from a normal sample of primary schools in the same region (not cited). Children are asked to rate which adults they admire most. The results are entertaining (politicians score rather more highly than their counterparts might in hypothetical Western surveys), but intriguingly indicative of differences in media literacy. The film course has pushed the visibility of symbolic heroism above the power of politics, and the experienced labour of parents and teachers. It has also downgraded the ordinary friendship of classmates. Given the emphasis that many teachers in the course laid on localised socialisation outcomes in the teaching, these outcomes are rather disappointing.

In Film Course schools, children most admired (in this order): politicians, movie stars, scientists, their fathers, and sports stars. In the non-Film Course schools, children cited their mothers, fathers, teachers, classmates, and politicians, (Shi, Lei, and Wang 2000). Students who had undergone intensive media study seemed to have caught the fame bug and were citing movie stars and sports heroes as major role models. The researchers do not explain how this sudden rush for celebrity aids children's socialisation, nor their physical and intellectual development. It would also be interesting to know, but not hard to guess given the Disney and revolutionary percentage in the available packages, how the Film Course managed to push mothers entirely out of frame.

The teacher's local results were more persuasive of the educational value taken from the Film Course. All the conference presenters, bar one Mainland and one Hong Kong participant, were female, either representative senior teachers, or teachers who had themselves managed the classroom teaching of the project. There was, therefore, a strong sense of female competency associated with the event, which was enhanced by the presence of Yu Lan as guest of honour. As in all international meetings, some teachers were initially nervous—or the equipment failed them—but overall the impression was one of commitment, differentiated and inventive teaching and learning, and talent finding a niche. The demise of the status of mothers in the admiration sample is perhaps a symptom, however, of the strong vein of patriarchy in children's film. If the titles which teachers referred to in their presentations were typical of school choices (*Robinson Crusoe, Gulliver's Travels, Snow White, Lion King*) then none of them honour motherhood!

Schools were offered 216 "packages" of available films. These were either thematic edited collections of films (dogs, monks,[23] witches, Pearl Harbor [!], outer space, pirates) or collections of films which have several versions: *Around the World in Eighty Days, Six Warring States (Zhanguo), Cinderella* (five of the available seventy-seven versions were selected for the course), *Tarzan* (twelve films), *Robinson Crusoe*, and *Gulliver's Travels*. Many of the films seem rather antiquated to the eyes of a Western film educator, but it must be remembered that the course intends to give students a context in which to place their film spectatorship generally. It is the modality of the teaching that makes this experiment interesting. There is a rather proscriptive system of film selection for the trial and presumably for the curriculum once it is in place. The slogan of the course is "Let Children See Only the Best Films!" which immediately introduces the canonisation of some texts over others. Films are required to be "classical" and to aid "psychological development" within an overall curricula remit to socialise the young. Nevertheless, the implementation of the programme at classroom level is undertaken by a large cohort of primary teachers who are mobilising this course for locally differentiated outcomes. The *Robinson Crusoe* story at the beginning of this chapter was a good example of local creative practice within an overall doctrine of socialisation, "quality," and controlled media literacy. Other examples from very different schools exemplify this further.

In Shenzhen, the Nanshan foreign languages school provides (almost) bilingual education to children of wealthy parents. The film project at Nanshan looked at *Gulliver's Travels* and used the semester to emphasise advanced literacy in English. Despite the "subject" rather than "comprehensive" focus (and potentially vocational focus of the work given the association of English with work opportunities) the project did promise a multi-modal delivery of the text. Classes were organised around six activities and facilitated by various media (word cards, VCR, VCD, microphone, microrecorder, paper, video camera). The activities took the students through the story sequence by sequence, and encouraged them to memorise the text through analysis, imitation, acting, and dubbing. The last activity was filmed so that the children again produced their own version of the film. The teachers also published a short booklet beautifully illustrated with drawings by children (mostly in *manga* style), and still images from a cartoon version. The project booklet promised that there would be social as well as subject outcomes to the learning process. "Students are very interested in acting. They'll feel themselves important through participation, they will gain confidence, and learn more from peers through cooperation."

At the Pingxiang experimental kindergarten, also in Jiangxi (Tang 2002), the Film Course was used to promote an environmental theme across the curriculum.

> We have only one earth to live on! (*renlei zhiyou yige diqiu*) The balance of nature has much to do with whether or not humankind and creatures can live together in harmony. In order to foster an awareness of environmental pro-tection (*huanbao yizhi*) from early childhood, and at the same time to de-velop a healthy life habits (*jiankang de shenghuo*) and behaviour patterns (*xingwei fangshi*), we have introduced motion pictures into our classroom un-der the direction of the taskforce of the National Science Education Program. (Tang 2002)

Again the work was tied to the current national push for "comprehensive" education within the ninth Five Year Plan, and to the functionality associated with science and technology. Students' favourites were a mixture of ani-mated Disney and Shanghai classics, all with an animal theme, and historical stories of heroic revolutionary children in the countryside. They included *Bambi* (Disney), *Little Tadpole* (Shanghai), *Sparkling Red Star*, *Dumbo* (Dis-ney), *Snow White* (Disney), *Lan Mao* (Blue Cat), and *Red Children (Hong Haizi)*. Animal survival, habitat, and child heroism (now redirected from *the* Revolution to a revolution in social attitudes to the world's resources) were emphasised in the readings of these films. Children engaged in role play and were taken outside the classroom to give out leaflets, clean up parks, erect posters, and to march in the streets of World Environment Day.[24] Although not described as "literacy," this use of films to further many social issues in the classroom is very much about promoting media literacy as a *functional* part of a comprehensive education.

The Film Course also highlighted the social revolution in parental choice in education, although it also helped unlikely schools to benefit from the caché of media in the classroom. Whilst some of the better equipped schools were chosen for the Film Course, so too were relatively remote schools in Guizhou. After the first year or so of the extra activity, parents tried to send children to schools particularly so that they could get the film "advantage." As examples of professional best practice, these (and there were several more) case studies had underlined the emergence of specialised teachers of multi-literacy and multi-modality in the service of the social *and* the modern imperatives. Further, whilst the initiatives do not challenge the highly sys-tematic political organisation underlying Chinese school curricula, they do suggest a willingness to allow children to work with a visual "package" in a local context. Shi's human nature model, and its attendant educational principles, point to a prescriptive version of socialisation, but Shi's memory of film as a formative influence on his youth also intimates a genuine desire to extend children's experience. In the classroom this kind of media literacy program can be exploited by clever and imaginative teachers to make learning part of a familiar world, one that is smaller than China, but greater than top-down modelling of social behaviour.

New media literacies do not offer a panacea nor a certain path anymore than did the left wing films that Yu Lan saw in Beijing, or the Chaplin movies that Xie Tian mimicked in Tianjin. They do not preclude such turns either. Competencies acquired through many modes of interlinked communications are a starting point for the expression of self, and of answering the questions, who am I and where am I going? How do I get there? They are also building blocks for emerging social individuals and groups whose maturity cannot be foreseen. The Ninth Five Year Plan to produce "comprehensive qualities" through education is to prepare China's next generation for an internationally oriented, economically dynamic, yet stable society. But, as Yu Lan and Xie Tian have themselves proved over almost a century of creativity, education produces people, not certainties.

NOTES

1. *A Brief Account of the China Children's Film Society* (2000) and personal discussions with Lin Amien, July 2002.

2. Conversation with Yu Lan, December 2000.

3. This is a common detour for young directors and one which irritates the Studio. As one studio director commented: "If Zhang Yimou hadn't come to us he'd have gone nowhere, no *Red Sorghum* (*Hong gaoliang*) without a *Red Elephant* (Hong xiang)!" (Zhang Yimou was responsible for the cinematography on *Red Elephant*. Zhang Jianya and Tian Zhuangzhuang directed.)

4. There is a vast literature on Chinese education. Reviews, historical analyses, and in-depth case studies include Kwong (1979); Barlow and Lowe (1987); Lee (1987); Hayhoe (1989; 1992); Rosen (1992; 1995); Lin (1993); Lee and Postiglione (1995); Ma (1995); Han (2001); Yang (2000a; 2000b); Beemer (2001); Feng (2001); Gu (2001); Tsang Mun (2001); Chao (2002); Cheng and Wong (2001).

5. A survey of the literature and evaluation of the social science instrument "Chinese Value Survey" developed by Bond, is given in Matthews (2000, 117–27).

6. An AAS panel of senior scholars debated the issue again in Washington, D.C., 2002.

7. Christiansen gives a figure for those unemployed or in other ways adversely affected by SOE reforms as thirty million (2002, 181).

8. Pricelessness is gender-specific in many areas. The gender ration rose from 104.9 in 1953 to 107.6 in 1982, and—nearly twenty years after the one child policy was introduced—rose again to 117 (117 boys registered for every hundred girls) (*Annals*, 18).

9. Xinhua News Agency. Accessed: 13 August 2002. www.cnd.org/Global/02/08/13/020813-93.html

10. This was a pre-census guesstimate quoted in Feng 2002, 30.

11. Source: *Annals* (2000).

12. It must be noted that this was already, however, a vast improvement on the late Republican figures. In 1937 a Fujian census showed all towns with a larger proportion of boys in the population. They outnumbered girls by two to one overall; in some towns the percentage was 77 boys to every 17 girls (*Annals* 2002, 12).

13. Discussed by Stefan Landsberger in a panel presentation on political iconography, AAS Washington, April 2002.

14. Wang Guangwu in a Radio Australia seminar at the Sydney Myers Asia Centre, Melbourne, 2002.

15. *Visual Communication* journal promotional material, 2002.

16. Argued for in documents prepared by the Lide Institute (2002), run by "patriotic entrepreneur," Zhang Junming.

17. Fan Wenfang, Tsinghua University.

18. For "foreign language" in these proposals, read "English."

19. Wang Liuyi—Wang 6/1 has a name that records his birthday on Children's Day, 1 June. His work in children's media seems therefore entirely appropriate!

20. 77,728 students and 4,144 teachers have taken part in fifty-six schools across fifteen provinces since the viability study in 1995.

21. Film Course details provided by Wang Liuyi. Interested readers can find more information at www.sunchime.com.cn.

22. Shi would be gratified to read that, in the impoverished Guizhou province, a village head arranged for all villagers to watch the donated films together with the children (Wang and Li 2000, 14).

23. We were pleased to see a class on the Shanghai Animation Studio film *Three Monks, Sange heshang* demonstrated at the conference—as it is a film we have used in focus group work amongst Chinese-Australians in Western Australia and also amongst schoolchildren in Beijing (Donald and Lee 2001).

24. Jane Sayers (2004) has argued in doctoral work that the sanctioned activities of environmentalists both draw on Maoist models of mass movements and mobilisation (*yundong*), whilst also inadvertently preparing young people for possible anti-state activities in the future. This argument is premised on the seminal Wasserstrom and Esherick article on student activism in Tiananmen (1991).

5

Creativity and National Style

CREATIVITY, DELIBERATION, AND THE INTERNET

In 1874, a newspaper for children was published in Guangzhou, The Child's Paper *(xiaohai yuebao). A newspaper for children is a great thing. Its presence in the market remarks on child literacy, child interests, and, crucially, hints at the possibility of children forming part of a public, visible, social sphere. There have been a host of subsequent publications, from the radical* Shanghai Youth Magazine *(Shaonian zazhi 1911) to the educational reform-based* Children's World *(Ertong shijie 1922), to the Shanghai weekly* Little Friends *(Xiao pengyou 1922), and many more, of which the 4 May movement's* New Youth *is probably the most well-remembered. The editorial statement of* Little Friends *declared that the publication wanted to foster "brave, active, happy, just and hard-working children." It lasted under three editors until 1966, when it closed, apparently due to the disruptions and uncertainties of the Cultural Revolution. It re-opened in 1978, publishing short stories, children's artwork, poems, songs, and general information.*

Specifically Party-oriented broadsheets and magazines were also widely distributed after 1949. Chinese Children *(Zhongguo ertong 1949) was founded shortly after Liberation. That only lasted until 1951, but meanwhile* Children's Century *(Ertong shidai 1950),* Good Children *(Hao haizi 1950), later* Red Children *(Hong haizi 1959), and* Little Red Guard *(Hong xiaobing 1974) and then* New Youth *(Xin shaonian 1978). The* China Youth Daily *(Zhongguo shaonian bao 1950) is still published, as are regular youth inserts into city papers, but children are more likely to cite the popular contemporary cartoon collection* Master Joker *(Youmo dashi) or a football monthly (if they can afford the cover price) as a favourite read.*

This historical snapshot supports the underpinning argument in this final chapter, that children in the Chinese media sphere have long been recognised as part of an economy of knowledge, albeit one based on national political coherence rather than the creative survivalism of market states in the West. The basis for this contention lies in a reevaluation of consumption and cosmopolitanism, which does not shy from the context of a strong state and an overtly politicised market environment. The argument does not pretend that the trajectory from *Little Red Guard* to *Master Joker* has been smooth. It does suggest, however, that the ways in which children are provided with, and use, media establish them as participants in a mediated and internationalised economy of knowledge. This observation is important for both studies of the media and for students of contemporary China. It attests to the readiness of Chinese children for the competitive media economies; both literal, the global markets, and imaginary, the international media imagination. In this chapter the focus is again mainly on visual media, film, and animation, but the claim goes further; that children are literate and cosmopolitan consumers whatever medium is in play. Creative literacy has been put forward as a tactic through which to avoid censorship and to facilitate agency amongst young media users (Guntarto 2001, 200). Thinking about children as creative consumers is a similar semantic move and it mobilises a potent terminology, excerpting the idea of agency as an intentional and socially directed competency, and suggesting that it can be twinned with the ideas of creative activity and communities of practice that are generated around children's media use worldwide and which can be transferred to debate Chinese media industries. The economy, the creativity of individuals and groups, and the consumption practices of people in society can be made coherent through such new paradigms of knowledge creation and deployment.[1]

Table 5.1 offers one account of an economy of media activity. It tells of the penetration and accessibility of different media technologies to urban teenagers in Beijing. Further data from the same survey suggests the time given to different media, in descending order of frequency: television, books, newspapers, recorded music, radio, magazines, computers, VCDs (film), videos, and finally the Internet. However, those figures indicate duration rather than intensity, and do not necessarily tell us much about user choice. Films on VCD and video may make a larger impression than the time spent in their consumption reveals, and indeed respondents in our own surveys back up the claim that film has a stronger affect than "cooler" media. Students in Hong Kong and Beijing have confirmed in interviews (2003) that the computer VCD format is preferred over television as the computer tends to be kept in the student's room, and is therefore more private than the television, which is shared by the entire family. The Internet also comes low on the list, but that may be because logging on was a luxury in China in 2000, as in many other parts of the developed world, although in this Beijing sample, the problems were mainly to do with access to servers rather than real infrastructural poverty. By 2003, Internet access nationwide had increased to 30 percent, with many of these connections in major cities. If we are interested in how the Internet inspires users, and what they do with it, usage needs to be taken in its own context, and not compared to more widely available media. A connected study of middle school students' preferred uses of the Internet showed a wide range of activities, with quite small differences in preference between each. "Communicating with friends" came out top, with "finding good sites for my friends and my own (pop) cultural interest" a close second, "making contact with international friends" (which could indicate direct contact or could just refer to overseas websites) third, and so on. The first seven categories were all related to communication with other people or with fan clubs. Study-related use came low down the list of options, except for study of aspects of the Internet itself.

The authors (CTRI 2000) concluded that media were changing the relationship between people in urban Beijing, allowing them to make friends across generations and to enhance friendship links within school environments. Students were using the technology made available to them for purposes of education to follow their own interpersonal relationships, to deepen and share local and international cultural interests; to "make" connections. In the terms of creativity the research edged towards defining children as creative agents in a mediated society, a definition that nearly approximates the symptoms of post-Fordist creative consumers as the cornerstone of a market state. A footnote to this is that in the post-SARS environment many students are relying on distance education technologies as a backup to contact education.

In terms of what the sample group were opting to do with the Internet, there is also a sense that the deliberative opportunities of mediated communications were being creatively exploited by schoolchildren. Deliberation is a buzzword in political and media theory. It is linked to working "grassroots" democracy, and is seen as a way of activating Habermasian and Rawlsian ideas of communicative action and public reason in practical politics and

Table 5.1.   Media Penetration in Beijing Metropolitan District, 2000–2001

Medium	Penetration Percent in Primary School-Age Households
Personal Computer	42.2 (of which 76 percent go online)
Television	98.3
Tape/CD Player	93.6
Telephone	84.6
Video Player	74.5
VCD/Karaoke Equipment	55.3

Source: China Teenage Research Institution, 2000.

civil society. Habermas' communicative action principle puts communication in the forefront of socio-political competency, and rationality is assumed. Rawls' public reason is grounded in agreed principles of social justice, political values, and the right to free enquiry, all working to the ends of rational self-management (Rawls 1997). Children's self-management is not generally included in either of these spheres of thought. However, a mediated arena such as an online chatroom is working in parallel to the élite economies of knowledge, and can host a category of deliberation that is both passionate and creative. To that extent, the creative communications of middle school children on the Internet in China are acting outside the bounds of the deliberative spheres in Chinese politics and sociality. Their conversations with friends are, one supposes, mainly intimate and unthreatening to the status quo, but their very decisions to use the medium in ways that step entirely outside the limits of regulated content are at least as daring as the deliberations of western élites in academia and politics.

Peter Dahlgren, a Habermasian who has a clear-sighted approach to both the promises and flaws of deliberative theory, reframes deliberation within a real world of political spin, imperfect media regulation, commercial imperative, and the "increasing fragmentation of the public" (Dahlgren 2002, 6). He queries the true believers' contention (11) that political conversation is the benchmark of a complete democratic individual, and gives credence to those that argue for more creative communications amongst the publics of modern democracies (9–10). Dahlgren summarises the qualitative differences between conversation and "discussion" and between opinion and knowledge. Drawing on these contentions, it is arguable then first, that consumer creativity works within a passionate (Mouffe 2000) field of engagement, but secondly, that this cannot be generated without competencies, and not within a society that is scared of politics. Nonetheless, it happens in the area of consumption and extra-institutional interaction. This is a contradictory position, but it indicates that a conceptual schism between authoritarian and liberal states does not necessarily imply that the competencies in one are less or inferior to the other, nor that passionate creative agency is entirely dependent on democratic media.

Likewise there has been passionate work by media producers who have been working in China for decades. These communities of practice underscore that even institutionalised media contribute to the formation of communities of use that have deliberative potential. Part of the work of these media practitioners grows out of a high expectation of child competencies and of their rights to what is similar to a mediated but not necessarily commodified publicness. At the most basic of levels, these practitioners recognise that children have generation-specific tastes that ought to be answered by adult content providers. Qin Yuquan, a children's film scholar and scriptwriter, is not a modern radical, nor would he expect his ideas to make an impact anywhere except perhaps in the meetings of the Children's Film Society. Yet he shows the passion for creative coherence that exposes the fault lines between past ideals, contemporary markets, and a stagnant economy of social meaning. He claims that there are six things wrong with children's film in China today:

1. The film-makers are interested in the art of the film, not in children. . . .
2. They make films only in order to make money. . . .
3. . . . or, in order to express their ideas on something in which children are not interested . . .
4. They don't really respect the children, so they think that they can make children happy by cheating. . . .
5. The films' settings are not appropriate for children's imaginations . . .
6. In sum, Chinese children's films place undue emphasis on the significance of a script, they don't work hard enough on the plots and storylines, so the conception tends to be too simple, and, as the little actors are too nervous, Chinese children's films aren't funny.[2]

Qin does admit that there are some good films in circulation, but the six problems he articulates add up to a fundamental problem. The film-makers do not respect the creativity of their audiences, and so fail to entertain, to inform, or to challenge in ways which intersect with the passionate engagement which the children need. A film-maker who appreciates the possibilities of a child's imagination and patriotism would offer a text that goes beyond the rules of adult deliberation and aesthetic form, towards the realm of the unexpected, the relaxed, the intense, and the funny.

CHINA BEST! ANIMATION AND NATIONAL STYLE (*MINZU SHI*)

"San Mao" has been my favourite character since I was very little. Whenever I see "San Mao," it reminds me of my childhood. Though the memories may seem vague, it brings back a sense of nostalgic feeling. . . .

I would like to make a movie about the Japanese invasion on China. I would make this movie dramatic and sensationalised. I would want this movie to be internationally famous. Some people may find this movie controversial and mentally numbing [meaning "horrifying"]. But the truth is the truth. (Wang Yan, R.1) (The comment was accompanied by a portrait of Sanmao entitled "China Best!" see figure 1.1.)

Nostalgia starts young! At thirteen years old, Wang Yan is still, formally, in childhood. His appeal to nostalgia conflates the longevity of Sanmao himself with a memory "though vague" of his own much more recent childhood. It is not clear in his responses whether he is referring to the modern *Sanmao in the Army*, the television series of Sanmao in the 1980s, or the original 1948 film. What is clear from Yan's illustration, however ("China Best!") is that part of the value of Sanmao lies in his quintessential Chineseness. As he goes on to describe the movie that he would make, it is also clear that Wang Yan's associative identification with Sanmao involves a declaration of patriotism. In the format of the questionnaire he manages to create an identification, which also communicates a great deal of national passion. His classmate, Zhuang Yaoji (12) gives an entirely different impression of media use. Her favourite film is a Disney live action family film, with spunky twin girls as the central characters. They help each other in a transatlantic plot to bring their parents together. The clinching scheme is floating the father's girlfriend out into the lake on a camping trip. Zhuang's favourite character is an "unconventional rabbit," and her own story idea is again about sisters helping each other out. Without follow up I can only guess that this one-child family girl would really like a sister, and is telling us this through a fantasy of rescue.

[My favourite film] is a movie called *Tian Sheng Yi Dui* (Born as a Pair/The Parent Trap). There were two little girls who looked alike. One only had a father; the other only had a mother. In the end, they found out they were twins and live together as a family.

[My favourite character is] a rabbit called "Bao Gei" (Eighth Brother) who enjoys eating carrots and has very long ears. He is very cute and confident. I admire and like him as he is unconventional and does unexpected things.

I like real life actors. They seem more personal and real. Occasionally, they appear more touching.

I would like to write a mythical story. The story tells of two sisters who find a mirror. One day, the older sister enters the mirror and finds herself lost in the "mirror's world." The young sister accidentally follows suit and is captured by a witch. The witch casts a spell on her, not allowing her to move. Under a fairy's supervision and help, the older sister manages to save her young sister and return home.

Yaoji is more concerned with the fantasy construction of the family than with Wang Yan's nostalgic and self-conscious patriotism. But, as Wang Yan obviously recognises, films about the Sino-Japanese war are not really the stuff of international television or film (although the U.S. film on Pearl Harbor made it into the Film Course lists).

As co-productions become more usual, so too does the need for workable intercultural themes. Almost all of the films at the 2002 International Festival of Children's Film (*Shandong*), contained an element of intercultural communication. Indeed, on the surface of the narratives, it appeared that many entries had not moved far from the 1958 China-France co-production model of *The Kite*. Children in one locale are magically removed to another. French children land up in Beijing, Innuit children in Iceland, Polish children find themselves on the Great Wall, and less obviously, but with equally dramatic potential, an urban Taibei boy discovers ghosts in the Taiwan countryside.[3] Whereas the 1958 show suggests a magical removal from one locale to another, the contemporary film migrations are much more aware of the real possibility of travel. Real planes, trains, and automobiles transport the travellers. The Innuit boy who walks across the ice and arrives in a superstitious community of Icelandic Christians is a true migrant. He has travelled before arriving, but on arrival his difference is not negotiable and his competencies are not recognised by his hosts. It is a children's film, so there is a happy ending; Norwegian trading boats arrive carrying an Innuit scout, the boy's father. He goes home to his family. The Taiwanese boy experiences urban-rural migration, and the dislocation of modernity. His parents are overseas and he is left with a grandmother who speaks Taiyü (not Mandarin, which he can understand), who has special relationships with the spirits, and whose pet cat turns into a monster (which the boy and grandma finally unite to defeat). These characters are all engaged in the trauma of translocal relationships, and the challenges of intercultural competency. Magic is mainly replaced by critical takes on superstition.

The children in the films at the festival are "co-production kids," necessarily cosmopolitan. They combine family drama with international travel (*The Parent Trap* twins jet from California to London and back again with consummate panache). Yet the patriotism of Wang Yan, and the great success of *Xi You Ji* (yet another version of *Journey to the West*) in 1999, suggests that national style should be cultivated even in a transnational marketing logic. The Disney studio knows children all over the world better than anyone else, but never gives up on its Americanness. That is the core of its identity as a production house. Children are increasingly cosmopolitan consumers, but this by no means precludes the attraction of familiarity, locality, and national style (*minzu shi*).

There is an argument (Gao 2001) that animators have long adapted narrative structures to accommodate fantasies of the moment, and that they have done so as an escape from ideology, whilst also commenting on politics. The

Table 5.2. Shanghai Fine Art Animation Production (including television animation) 1940–1994

	1940s–1950s	*1960s*	*1970s*	*1980s*	*1990–1994*
Number	68	53	42	193	83
Total Duration (min)	1450	1230	1280	3620	1510
Average Duration (min)	21	23	30.5	19	18

Source: Adapted from (Gao 2001, 21–61). The duration shows the effect of reform era (opening up to foreign product) and of television scheduling on 1980s production. By 1994 there is still no sign of the Chinese made feature length animation characteristic of Disney product. In 2004 the situation has not changed, except to see a further decrease in animation production in national studios.

effect of the animation is to intensify the appeal to structures of fantasy in the social world, but at the same time to make those structures strange. The effect in a truly excellent animation may be widespread popularity—as in the case of *Journey to the West*. It may be one of multiple fantasy options as in *Three Monks* (*Sange hezhang* 1980, Dong Nianxi).

Three Monks is a prescribed text for the Chinese Primary initiative of the Film Course, it is also a film cited by thirty-something Chinese-Australian migrants as a film they cherish from their youth (Donald and Lee 2001). In focus groups in Perth, the film was described by adults as about Sino-Japanese relations, and by a young boy as insulting to Buddhists. In the Film Course it was cited as a film that promotes moral cooperation, and also a film that uses sparse draughtsmanship to suggest classical figurative art and brushwork styles. The story is simple. A small monk lives alone in a temple at the top of a steep hill. Every day he descends the hill to collect water from the lake. One day, a tall thin monk joins him. At first they share water and food, but trouble arises from the question of who is to collect the water. A fat monk then arrives and causes yet more trouble by his extreme thirst and laziness. They all sulk, the temple becomes tinder dry, the bodhisattva weeps. Then the temple mouse knocks over a candle and a fire takes hold. Now the monks must fight the flames. After some trial and error they work out a fair way of sharing the labour, and beat the fire down. The following day they devise a trolley system from the top of the hill, and thus resolve the problem. Technology triumphs.

Three Monks has only a music soundtrack and three main characters (plus the mouse). In the classroom, children were asked to act out the parts, and describe their contribution to the problem and the solution. Rather sadly, a noticeably fat child was expected to play the fat monk. Perhaps this was a little too realistic. Clearly the film was used in the class to make some points about style, and to drive home the moral of the tale: cooperation, technology, and compromise are the way of the future. All the children understood this and made the appropriate points in their role play. It was an instance of directive moral consumption, linked, however, to visual literacies and thereby to the assumptions of creativity in a national economy of knowledge. This animation was made on the cusp of reform era and the influx of mainly American and Japanese imports. It bears no trace of *manga* style, nor of Disney, both of which (with their leaders, Mickey Mouse and Atongmu) had already entered the television market. By the time it was used in classroom teaching in 1995–2000, it still offered an effective vehicle for children's fantasy (funny characters, selfish adults, and a naughty mouse), but in many aesthetic respects it had become a relic of an almost forgotten national style.

The first full length animation television feature, *Lotus Lantern* (*Bao lian deng*, Shanghai, 1999) has been critically praised but also acknowledged as derivative of Disney's style, and comparable with *The Lion Kong* (*Shizi wang*).⁴ The conception of the non-Han characters is also suggestive of Disney's *Pocahontas*, although one could also argue that its focus on dance and song also draws on deeply rooted media versions of minority peoples in China. These forays into feature-length animation challenge the dominance of international style but also accommodate it. The sophistication of animation has not yet outgrown its associations with cartooning and childishness, however.

> I like life-like characters. When I was young, Daddy would let me watch cartoons. However, as I grew older, Daddy didn't like me watching cartoons as he felt they were for "babies" to watch. Once when I watched cartoons Daddy scolded me and said I was "useless." As I didn't want to be "useless," I stopped watching cartoons. Since then, I have had a greater fascination for life-like characters than for animated cartoon characters. (Wang Yan, 13)

Zhu Xiao-ou, of the Love Children Film and Television Society, would support Wang Yan's original love of cartoons as an appropriate component of a child's media experience. She goes so far as to promote the idea of films that combine live action and animation as the best way to communicate with the young. This is not a new idea in film or television (from *Bedknobs and Broomsticks* to *Saturday Disney*) but one that is cutting edge in a media environment once predicated on a separation of realism and fantasy, with both subject to ideological constraints. "Children like cartoons. . . . They like the overstatement, the distortion and the humour, the expansiveness of cartoons." Zhu is refreshingly nonjudgemental on the modes and subjects of media content, arguing that children's media have changed both in relation to changing times and in the context of a changing adult industry. This is not a problem for Zhu. She divides children's film into those that were made with an ideal of education for society, and those that contribute towards children's personal happiness and development, and suggests that both have historical value.

> Chinese children's films have changed just as Chinese cinema has changed. The most apparent difference is a shift in thinking. The traditional notion of children's film was that national and revolutionary traditions should be used as a basis from which to educate children. The classic films all achieve this: *Little Soldier, Zhangga* (*Xiaobing zhang ga*), *Chicken Feather Letter* (*Jimao xin*), *Red Children* (*Hong haizi*), and *Sparkling Red Star* (*Shanshan hongxing*) pay attention to revolutionary narratives, whilst cartoons such as *The Magic Paintbrush* (*Shenbi Maliang*) care much more about national traditions. The characters in these films gave a kind of purity to the children's cinema. But there are also disadvantages. When I was a child I liked these films, and so did other children. But the reforms have changed children, and given them wider perspectives than they had in the past. As a result, they want films that will bring them hope and hap-

piness, and which feed their imaginations. They really want to see films, watch television, all of that. But adults aren't much good at communicating with children. So children don't like the films that they make. Film producers don't understand children's tastes. Children like ideas that run fast and without too strong a sense of order imposed on them, they are not interested so much in a conclusion as in a wonderful story along the way. But adults tend to take a very familiar story and re-tread it as a vehicle for education. They are always looking back at history and emphasising education through tradition. At least they were. In the current period children's filmmakers are beginning to pay more attention to fun and enjoyment. [It seems to me that] Chinese children like the naughty characters who resist their parents. In the past child characters suffered as a way of educating the audience. Children didn't like them, they just watched them suffer. Now the films tell stories about normal children living in normal families. And they tell stories that show that children can make the world better. They also try to create an aesthetic awakening in children, to enlighten children's hearts. Think about *Thatched Roof* (*Cao fangzi*), that is so beautiful. (Zhu Xiao'ou 2002)

Despite her protestations Zhu Xiao'ou also has a pronounced educational imperative in her perfect film. She sees room for normality, for children's agency "making the world better," and for beauty. However, her ideas are courageous, insofar as she wants to see films let go of history and to take a few leaps into a less calculated present. She places a difference between revolutionary patriotism and the national style (*minzu shi*), the "China Best" of Sanmao. Changes are necessary for the affectivity, market viability, and functionality of films if her vision is to succeed. She notes that, whilst *Thatched Roof* did well in foreign film festivals, it did not get a release in the domestic market. Cinema distributors are nervous of children's film produced domestically because it has a bad reputation amongst children themselves. Zhu also surmises, and her opinion is borne out by the responses to our questionnaires, that children want to see stories about resourceful, intelligent children who can make a difference for themselves and other people. This does not automatically mean Chinese children, however, although it does for Wang Yan. Where once that child might have been embodied in the revolutionary courage of Shanshan or Zhangga, s/he is now quite possibly foreign, inhabiting a fantasy world that is created from the literature, dreams, and imaginations of other traditions and other worlds. "I would like to produce a children's movie about China's history and culture. I would use cartoon animations in this movie. I would talk about China's long history of five thousand years, her scenic views. This movie would be easily understood and relaxing" (Wu Zhu Gei 11).

Zhugei's history, culture, and landscape film needs a bit of development, but the idea—which she may have moved onto—of superimposing cartoon versions of Chinese historical figures and cultural icons onto live action backdrops of Chinese landscapes, might work. Animation in China has exemplified a national style (*minzu shi*), whilst also being subject to ideological control. As Zhu Xiao'ou hints in her assessment of animation (*The Magic Paintbrush*), there has always been room for ideological escape in the guise of the first priority of national style. Animators have used their fine art and crafts skills to develop and support "ethical narrative tactics." One such is the "tragic hero," a cipher in the structure of Chinese tragedy (*Zhongguo beiju lunli moshi*). Gao Fang argues that this hero is a national invention, a hero that has no fatal flaw, but yet fails at the very end to destroy evil in others (Gao 2001, 47–48). She cites *Nezha Stirring Up the Sea* (1979) and *Storm in Heaven* (1964) as typical examples. The point is that such classical accounts of failure could be countenanced in animation, where in live action they could not.

COSMOPOLITANISM: CHOOSING (HAI)-LI-PI-TE

"He Li Pi Te is intelligent, courageous and helpful. That's why I like him."

—Mao Yijie, 10

The contradictions behind the tastes and preferences of the child audience demonstrate a tension between national preference and internationalised taste. Future research would require a longtitudinal content analysis of media coverage and of promotional materials, and a playground ethnography of peer pressure. That has not yet been possible (and it would have had to be done in hindsight), but the arguments here are based on collect comparative opinion over a reasonable range of sources. The children surveyed in the 2000, 2001, and 2002 research came from Beijing, Shanghai, Shenzhen, Jiangsu, and Zibo. They were aged between eight and fifteen years old. Some had had the advantage of being involved in the Film Course experiment previously described. Some were located in rural schools, others were in university schools and therefore enjoyed a strong intellectual catchment. There were outstanding contributions from some children, both on paper and in discussion groups. Some have already been quoted. Overall, children expressed firm opinions, with younger children tending to be more impressed with recent television and film, whilst older children—with the advantage of hindsight and nostalgia—were more particular. In 2000, boys wanted to talk about Pokémon, and girls thought they were silly. In 2001, when we were testing an English language CD-ROM with parents and children, there seemed to be overwhelming evidence that *Hello Kitty* and *Totoro* (H. Miyazaki) had conquered the girls' imaginations. Even in Children's Day schoolwork exhibitions, most computer-generated essays were accompanied by downloaded images of these virtual Japanese muppets. But in 2002, there was the strongest evidence of a non-Japanese foreign import making a profound impact on children's tastes.

It was a dusty and hot July day in Beijing at the Tsinghua middle school. The classroom was full of children waiting for the last bell so they could leave and get on with their summer holidays. Grade 5-6 students had been asked to hang back for one last session, a meeting with a foreign researcher who wanted to ask them about their favourite movies. The children agreed to do so, they were in any case quite proud of the questionnaires that they had already completed—full of pictures of favourite characters, and comments on the kinds of film that they would make if they had an opportunity to do so. The researchers were aware that some of their parents and grandparents were waiting for them outside in the sun and that it wouldn't be fair to make this session go on for too long. Once the conversation started it was, however, difficult to stop. The children were falling over themselves to tell the researchers that their favourite film of all time is *He Li Pi Te*. The main character was "brave" and "intelligent" and they all admired him.

This was only the second focus group of the year, and the first conversation in which this film had been raised as a topic. At first the foreign researcher was surprised. She had misheard *He-Li-Pi-Te* as *Hai-Li-Bu* and was amazed that the children were citing it with such passion, although secretly pleased too as this would mean that Shanghai animation still worked for the young Chinese consumer. *Hailibu* is an animation short classic from the mid-1980s and tells of a boy whose kindness to a woodland animal brings him the gift of speaking with beasts. The condition for this gift is that he must never divulge it to other people. If he does so he will be turned to stone. The boy is a member of a nomad tribe. One night, as the people are partying under the stars, the animals in the holding pens grow restless. They tell Hailibu that a huge flood is coming and that he must release them and warn his tribe. He tries to do so but is not believed. Eventually he tells his elders where the information has come from, and, as the people flee panic-stricken from the oncoming disaster, Hailibu turns to stone. The film ends with the people's plaintive cry in his honour: "Haiii—Liiiii—Buuuuu!"

The reason this film would have been an interesting choice for the children is that it is an old-fashioned, but elegant, animation that achieves nicely a blend of adventure, fantasy, and patriotism (*ai guo*), whilst also including a minority people into a national mythology of self-sacrifice and loving the people (*ai min*). Had they really chosen this film then there would have to be some purchase in an argument that foreign media content and merchandising impact had not dented the national inclinations of the young generation and that education methods were still producing patriots in primary schools. Given that Hailibu displays a love of people but is also susceptible to gifts from a woodland god, it could be argued that the film combines national content with patriotism in a manner that supports revolutionary ideals.

Of course, they were actually referring to the international children's hit of 2001, *Harry Potter and the Philosopher's Stone* (Columbus). The enthusiasm for Harry and Hermione emerged as the session went on, and became clearer still as we later compared fifty-eight questionnaires submitted by other children from four provinces and metropolitan centres (Shandong, Jiangxi, Beijing shi, Shanghai shi) and several schools. In answer to question four, "Draw a picture or write a few words about your favourite film character," thirty-six different characters were mentioned. Harry and Hermione had ten hits. Other recent international releases (*A Bug's Life*, *The Lion King*) scored 4–6 mentions. Mickey Mouse, Donald Duck, and Goofy also scored in this range. There were one or two mentions of Japanese animation television characters (Atongmu, Sakoro Mamoto); the male lead, Liu Zhenhan, in a 2000 film about corruption in Chinese society; Monkey (Sun Wukung) and Piggy (Zhu Bajie) from *Journey to the West* (*Xi You Ji*); and some classic film figures: Sanmao, and Little Soldier Zhangga. What we drew from this eclectic list and the discussions we had with the children in focus groups was a sense that there is a broad and deep commitment to character in children's media. This commitment is attracted to immediate memory and the fashion factor, which must in part account for the prevalence of Harry/Hermione choices, but it also evidences a selective approach to classic films, to television content, and to video releases. As with all questionnaires, some answers drew more qualitative attention than others.

One twelve-year-old cited the 2000 animation feature *Lotus Lantern*, and drew a storyboard of key scenes to explain the story.[5] She remembered that her mother had taken her to see it and gave the distinct impression that it was the film's quality but also the theatrical experience of seeing the film with her mother that had enriched the attachment. She also comments that her best films are otherwise foreign-made (in which she includes Disney's Mulan, who is her favourite character). She feels that Chinese films tend to be too focused on education (*jiaoyu*), apparently differentiating here between entertainment as an end in itself and socialisation as a primary motivation for media content. This respondent is gifted as a writer and artist and that helps her articulate her complex relationship with film. It is, for her, a self-conscious experience of identification and modelling, a narrative template through which to explore her own gifts as an artist, a mediated embodiment of her relationship with her mother, and a locus at which she examines the concept of foreign (*waiguo*) entertainment as opposed to national educative imperatives.

This young person is a complex consumer who helps us move forward in our understanding of children as media users in an international context. Her responses draw on local competencies (the style of draughtsmanship in her storyboard is absolutely in the realm of Shanghai animation with an added touch of Japanese *manga*/animé in the wide eyes of the small boy), but she has used them as a springboard from which to evaluate the pleasures of foreign texts. Unsurprisingly perhaps, Disney's "bridge" to the Chinese and Asian American child, Mulan, is a favourite. Mulan is both Chinese and

American, modern and traditional, filial and headstrong, the girl next door across two continents. She is local and translocal. She has been created, in the terms of the argument here, as a cosmopolitan product. The skill with which Mulan is consumed by the present respondent, and by other young girls the world over (Donald and Lee 2001), likewise arises as a cosmopolitan competency built on a sophisticated attraction to both the known and the merely visible in children's film. This demands not "just" a cultural competency, but one that requires shifts between political understanding and loyalty, between consumption-based value judgements and locally organised socio-political perspectives. It also requires, not an internationalist perspective, but a flexible "foreign" (*waiguo*) sense of the local. There are two versions of the cosmopolitan working in this case, the designer transethnic cartoon character whose moral narrative fits Chinese and American family values, and the child consumer, who calls on translocal selves to enjoy and evaluate international and domestic media product. Children's tastes as arbiters of cultural worth challenge adult pretensions to managing children's consumption. The self-confidence with which our respondent explained her relationship to favourite products was not that of a dupe or victim, but nor was it an entirely powerful position.

In this presentation of qualitative data I am mimicking to some extent the social scientific resources of the Film Course Chinese researchers. But I am also tangential in my readings. I want to underscore particularly the claim for children as cosmopolitan consumers. Children as consumers demonstrate a flexible understanding of national loyalty, aesthetic taste, and brand apprehension. In the study, children's responses to questionnaires, their discussions in focus groups, and the evidence of their consumer participation and access patterns at home and at school strongly suggests that the taste cultures in and through which they consume media product reveal amongst other things an exploratory and translocal imagination. The children surveyed were in the main children with a relatively affluent lifestyle, certainly in supposed comparison to children in impoverished rural areas. Whilst it cannot be proven here, I would, however, not want to rest the claim of sophisticate and cosmopolitan on that urban or affluent context. The contention is that children's flexible subjectivity is partly evidenced by their capacity to consume across boundaries of meaning, and that this capacity can be described within the rubric of what I call here cosmopolitan affect.

LEAVING OUT: CHILDREN'S CONSUMPTION ON THE MARGINS OF ANALYSIS

Children's consumption of media culture is generally located in a discussion of educational value, psychological harm or benefit, or cultural history.

Occasionally, and especially in the works of Buckingham (1999; 2000); Gauntlett (1996); Goonasekera et al. (2000); and Livingston (2002) there is also a real consideration of children's political potential and social status in respect to their use of media. The latter set of arguments derives from a heightened and appropriate expectation of child intelligence, social sophistication, and agency in the mimetic and negotiatory process commonly called growing up. The idea of children and citizenship has been canvassed, for example, as something that requires mediation if children are to have a visible stake in everyday worlds of meaning. It has been cited in this book as related to the quality (*suzhi*) of children and the rights discourse that surrounds their education and cultural value in China. Children and news has also been researched as a catch-all that underlines the importance of child visibility in the discourses and story structures that perform the making of history in national settings. Some of that research is not much more than a content analysis of "how many stories" and is only a first step on the road to useful analysis. Nonetheless, the fact that this research has been performed attests to the recognition of children's interests as topics within the communicative sphere, and that is not a small achievement. The connections between children as subjects and children as audience segments, as well as children as components of a protected audience, have been noted and in some cases developed into policy statements. Arguably, however, the adult anxiety, which informs so much in this field, can work here too. Are we giving them enough? Of the right kind of material? What is good television? Are we the only ones who can define that . . . through a regulatory body? Questions that have to be asked and answered by those who are research active but also politically astute, but questions nonetheless that slip easily towards moralism and imaginative and class-ridden constraint. In this research environment, children remain as targets, victims, or beneficiaries of adult creative decisions.

There are, however, film-makers worldwide making films that speak to and about children, and which also claim artistic credibility. The use of film noir pastiche in *Babe* was cited on a CCTC6 discussion of children's film as an example of excellent film-making and story-telling. Children's international film festivals are supported by UNESCO and by industries and government organizations, but are seldom highlighted in mainstream art press or in academic film debates. Children's cinema is the one area of film studies that turned to contextual, political, and psychological (if not phenomenological) methods and aims before thinking about a textual or psychoanalytical approach. Scholarly textual readings are few and intercultural comparisons even fewer. This may be because, I would suggest, traditional film studies involve an acknowledgment of the spectator as a psychoanalytically defined subject, and that is not a category usually extended to include children. This idea of nondefinition has indeed been brilliantly explored in children's literature and television: Philip Pullman's Christian epic *Northern Lights* (part one of the Dark Materials trilogy) defines children as flexible subjectivities with transforming daemons (souls) to prove it (and, as I have suggested, draws heavily on J. M. Barrie's *Peter Pan* and C. S. Lewis's Narnian Chronicles to achieve the narrative), whilst the children's versions of Monkey (*Xi you ji, Journey to the West*) and the Pokémon series are based on notions of transformation and trickery as the core survival skills of children in a fixed and unforgiving adult world. Ideally, as there does seem to be a theoretical case to be made that children's subjectivities are different from those of adults, this should pose a challenge to film scholarship rather than cause a refusal to engage.

The exception to the silence arises in the world of animé where Japanese auteurism works in a medium aimed at a cross-generational audience. Hasao Miyazachi (*Princess Mamamoto, Totoro*) is the obvious example. The generous artistry of his films confuses adult expectations in Western critical culture. In this case the response tends to mimic that made to TV shows that catch the popular wave; so, the artistic merit and depth of the works is considered or critiqued in the light of a cult take-up of the product, which in itself explains or categorises its cultural value for *adults*. This happened with *Teletubbies* (BBC/Ragdoll 1997) and is underway with Miyazaki's 2002 film, *Spirited Away*, also a film where children have access to other worlds and other personae. The centrality of adult taste structures to the evaluation of worth and value underlies this response. Children's choices as consumers of discretion are not considered enough to prove cultural worth (although they do, of course, direct marketing decisions).

COSMOPOLITAN AFFECT

If children pose a problem to film analysis due to their phenomenological flexibility on the one hand, and their pre-Freudian subjectivity on the other, they are even more challenging to geopolitical categories of personhood. The responses of teenagers and even younger children suggest the effectiveness of national socialisation in China, placing consumerism firmly in the context of patriotic affect and even something akin to brand loyalty. The internationalisation of children's taste is therefore hard to theorise as a cultural triumph of the West. The question I raise here is whether children's media tastes form a symptomatic example of a cosmopolitan affect that does not entail an antinational personal agenda. The cosmopolitan sophisticate is popularly a figure of limited value; a traveller with boundless cultural and social capital, a bon viveur with an extensive repertoire of tastes and a prodigious stomach for difference. The cosmopolitan hovers above the places in which she lives, unless of course those places are London, Paris, New York, or Shanghai, in which case she is not an unusual creature. The sophistication of the cosmopolitan is tautologous in this description.

Contemporary readings of the cosmopolitan are less exclusive and more focused on a broader claim to a political competency and relevance. The recognition of forced and necessary migrancy for large groups, the overarching impact of global flows in markets and labour dependency, and the perceived need to reach for a political agenda that works to check the demands of sovereign national priorities combine to produce a much more nuanced and complex version of the cosmopolitan. The "critical cosmopolitan" (Robbins 1998a, 8) that is fought over, for example, in the American academy (Robbins 1998b, 246–48), has to be both situated in local experience (only just escaping authenticity), and yet aspire to worldly cross-border relevance and comprehension. A new cosmopolitan may colloquially be nowhere at all; a global consumer with a gold frequent flyer card, but she may also and more interestingly be a person who can be both here and there without too excruciating a sense of irony and compromise. Or indeed a person, a Filipina maid in Hong Kong or an Iraqi refugee in an Australian detention camp, who must feel that compromise deeply but has little choice other than to play it through. For that last group the leap to a cosmopolitan consumer might appear forced and thoughtless, but being both here and there is increasingly common, if highly differentiated by privilege, and consumption is a significant performative aspect of that being.

These quasi-hypothetical cosmopolitans are not the subject of this discussion and have not been done descriptive justice here. They are suggested tentatively as comparisons to the cosmopolitan child consumer, an alternative, emerging category of competent who manages without physical access to the whole world. What are her credentials? This cosmopolitan is reduced but also expanded. S/he has an affinity with a nation-state but may not reside there. S/he has affective engagements, financial, cultural, forced, chosen with other places, and those other places are both known and imagined locations, Hong Kong, London, Hollywood, and also symbolic sites that qualify the outside world, the *waiguo*. This cosmopolitan makes real demands on both known and imagined places. S/he wishes to live in them, consume their products, and occupy their symbolic spaces. S/he wishes therefore to enjoy, or is forced to suffer, the affect of other places outside the local, which is or could once have been her national or subnational imagined home. Most of all, this cosmopolitan cannot ground her subjectivity in a fixed expectation of place or ethnic centrality. She is not fixed, her daemon must change to circumstance. Perhaps the chief of sorrows for this cosmopolitan is that she is hard to decipher, that she herself disappears—or becomes contradictory—on contact with the affect of being outside, *waiguo.*

Cosmopolitan affect is thus a descriptor for the engagement between the person or group and the idea of *waiguo*, the outside-countries and the not-home. It is achieved through the shock of being somewhere else, or through the imaginative effects of consumption of ideas and goods that suggest somewhere else. Whereas the cosmopolitan has heretofore been either an idealist or a leech, now the cosmopolitan is a symptom of global trade, of international communications, and of communicative competency in a complex mediated global environment. "I feel watching TV is a kind of pastime, but it's seeing film that is a kind of enjoyment" (Tu Zimu, 13).

Going to the movies is more or less of a commonplace depending on where you live. Only 60 percent of our respondents had seen films in a cinema, the vast majority saw them through VCD copies on their televisions at home. In China the cinema is a treat; with entry prices of 10–15 yuan it is not a quick decision on a rainy afternoon. VCDs are, however, very cheap (10–15 yuan), and pirated versions even cheaper (about 5 yuan).[6] Films specifically made for children are, in any case, given tiny releases and are generally distributed through schools, videos, and festival circuits. Moreover, large Warner Brothers style cinema complexes are not evident in most cities (although new agreements between Datuan and Warner distributors will alter that situation in 2005–2006). The popcorn-and-air-conditioning factor is about all the average cinema has to offer. Perhaps because of this limited range and availability, the kind of "enjoyment" offered by film is related to the extra excitement of a theatrical experience, the event, which that outing signifies, and the expectation of something different from television.

The nature of affect in cinema is much to do with the scale and quality of a theatrical projection. In *Harry Potter* the Quidditch match is rather like the Pod Race in the third *Star Wars* film; it's a computer game with a bigger backstory. As the rest of the drama is in both cases rather lamely performed, the set piece sparks an immediate response in the games-literate audience, who find in these sequences a generic structure through which to empathise with the screen characters with whom they expect to identify: Luke Skywalker and Harry Potter. The elevation of the sequences from game to affective passage relies in part on the dramatis personae, and in part on the sheer scale of the visual experience. In Philip Noyce's *Rabbit Proof Fence,* Australian children could watch indigenous Australian children in extreme close-up, and notice the beauty that is afforded and highlighted by this type of cinematic treatment. In an early sequence, as the three children are eluding the Tracker by moving upriver, there is a hiatus as each child's face is caught against the extreme blue of the Western Australian sky, as they listen for danger they are also beautiful. Beauty as affect has something to do with narrative but much more to do with the sophistication of child spectators who understand and respond to the codes and conventions of storytelling on film, and whose sophistication makes a cosmopolitan enjoyment of the film possible. The transfer of the child audience from white Australian to cosmopolitan Australian is achieved by affect. The impact of this in an explicitly political film, such as *Rabbit Proof Fence*, is that children as audience are actively engaged in a mediated deliberative engagement with Australian history and current political scandals. This could be constructed as an example of cultural citizenship—whereby a child is engaged in the debate, even if not able to respond in overt political forums.

In 2002 at the Zibo International Film Festival, the Icelandic-Canadian production *Ikingut* (*Friend*), telling the story of a little Innuit boy, was screened at 10:00 AM on an extremely hot July day, with temperatures outside the cinema at 42 degrees Celsius. The cinema was air conditioned and full to bursting with school children bussed in from around the city to see the film. They were excited and a little apprehensive. Each school child would get to see one film in the festival, but it was potluck which they caught. As the film opened on a long slow shot of ice and snow, and as the plot began with a little white boy witnessing debates on religion and superstition in a small Icelandic community, the audience grew restless. Twenty minutes in they were, collectively and completely, bored. Then, finally, a new character arrives on screen wrapped in white fur. The Icelanders at first think him a daemon. When he is revealed as a small (Innuit) boy, new troubles erupt in the community of the film. In the Zibo cinema his revelation as an Innuit caused another eruption. The children breathed a sigh of relief, "Look he's Chinese!" they called and whispered to one another, suddenly engrossed and exuberant at once.

These children were ordinary Zibo kids with only provincial access to VCDs, cinema releases, and television specials. Some may have been on the Film Course. But they too exhibited a cosmopolitan competency in their reception of the film. They worked from a local familiarity to engage with a deeply foreign text. The affect of the close-up of a Chinese-seeming face worked in an opposite direction from the affect of Molly, Daisy, and Grace in *Rabbit Proof Fence*. There, the intensity of vision created beauty, which in turn forced recognition from the audience as the familiar became strangely affecting. In *Ikingut*, the close-up was a revelation of desired familiarity, which banished the strangeness of the film up to that point. The success of that engagement was rooted in a sense of locality, which was available through the little boy. He looked Chinese but was clearly comfortable in the ice and snow of the Icelandic environment. He was recognisable to the audience (or so they thought) but he was also a stranger in a strange land on their behalf. As such he fulfilled the necessary credential of a cosmopolitan affect, he was here and there, friend and stranger, not at home but nonetheless visibly competent in this environment. The audience took their cue from the text and were similarly competent for the remainder of the film.

COSMOPOLITICS AT HOME

Research projects into children's consumption patterns, choices, and responses, as well as studies of levels of child visibility, participation, and access in mainstream media, combine in a statement of the child as a cultural citizen, or its local equivalent, across the world. Where consumption is low or access to news coverage impossible, then children are equivalently disadvantaged with adults. Where consumption is a sign of economic and political activity, children are involved participants. Children's consumption is dependent on adult gatekeepers to be sure, but that only makes them more adept in the creation of choices, the negotiation of meaning, and the appropriation and manipulation of structures of feeling derived from those practices. Studying children's consumption is hopefully, therefore, an intervention into political and social constructions of the child in the world. That the child is a consumer at all could be written off as a fact of globalisation, a symptom of exploitation of the young, and a tragedy to be managed by regulators. The child consumer is a global phenomenon and access to global goods is given in exchange for a certain, limited version of value.

The idea of the cosmopolitan consumer mooted here does not flinch those realities, but it does try to give credit to what people do, and what they have to negotiate in order to participate in the creative economies of international exchange. The children that I have cited above are participating in what Spivak has called the "gap," the hyphen of the nation-state (Spivak 1998, 334). For Spivak the gap is dangerous, it makes room for fundamentalisms and spaces of profound unfriendliness. In political terms in China, that unfriendliness could have long-term consequences for the state's survival. Even to acknowledge the possibility of the gap is confrontational in this sphere. To define a space between the state and the nation is already to deny the Party an absolute hold over the modern encounters between national feeling and governmental power. More profoundly the gap releases a space between the idea of Chineseness, and the many other definitions of ethnicity, culture, and history, which make up the experience of peoples living within China's geo-political borders. So, the "gap" of internationalised children's consumerism should be understood as relatively mild cosmopolitics. Children occupy the gap as a place from which to encounter other zones of meaning and competence, but not to challenge the assumed relationship between national coherence and Chineseness, with central power. In the gap they are certainly working with structures of feeling and narrative that have been defined and developed outside the boundaries of state discourse but they have not eluded the nation; they are still local, their Chinese loyalty is in no doubt. If the state ultimately loses the conceptual battle to marshall the idea of China, then these children might be ready to understand what change is possible. But meanwhile, the internationalisation of media does not intimate any necessary alteration in their loyalties. They love Mickey Mouse, and they admire Harry Potter, but give no indication that such pleasures in any way undermine their domestic political allegiances. China Best!

Cosmopolitics has always been with us but is now at the sharp end of debate on our rights and duties as strangers and friends, whether here or there. Jacques Derrida's coupling of cosmopolitanism and forgiveness, two talks collected in a slim volume, epitomises the ethical challenges of modern societies. Cosmopolitanism, says Derrida, was once about all the cities of the world. Now it is about "the city of refuge." Derrida ties the new cosmopolitanism firmly to a duty of hospitality (Derrida 2001). Hospitality is a long way from the dangers of fundamentalist politics, and national schisms. It is perhaps a more positive way to envisage the effects and affect of children's media consumption. It is foolish to assume that global media—regulated, marketised, profit-driven, and ideological—will lead any charge for political change in China or elsewhere. What they may facilitate is a facility of mind and feeling in young people, which could in turn allow a little creative hospitality towards the beauty of strangers and the adventures of the enemy.

If the child conceived as a cosmopolitan consumer has a political edge, I would wish that it is this hopeful one. If the child can find the hyphen between nation and state, and the flexibility of soul or daemon to find the hyphen between *waiguo* and at-home, then maybe the imaginative pass to hospitality will not be such a tremendous challenge as it appears to be for current adult generations, in China and elsewhere.[7]

NOTES

1. The ideas for this chapter were partly inspired by conversations produced by the Australian Research Council project; Internationalising the Creative Industries; China; and the WTO.

2. Interview with the author, 10 July 2002, Beijing.

3. *Grandma's Ghosts*, Rice Films (Taibei), 1999.

4. See: "Lotus Lantern and the Lion King" in *Chinese Television* 2000, chapter 1, (Gao 62).

5. Respondent 47, 2002.

6. Current prices, 2002.

7. China Teenage Research Institute 2000.

Appendix

NOTES ON METHOD

The interview data referred to throughout this book draw almost entirely on interviews with urban children and can only be taken to represent that segment of modern China.

Empirical research for this book has been pursued within several interlinked studies of media and children in China and in the Chinese diaspora. The material has been gathered over five years, 1998–2002. The preparatory fieldwork was carried out amongst adults and children in Beijing, who were asked in a street survey (seventy respondents) to identify the media that they most associated with childhood. Similar questions were asked at CCTV, at the Children's Film Studio, and in schools. This was pursued in Western Australia (WA), where there is a high population of recent (post-1989) Mainland Chinese migrants. Adverts and tear-out questionnaires were placed in the Chinese language newspaper in Perth, WA (*Australian Chinese Times*, ed. Zhang Ye). There were about forty responses in Chinese and English. Follow-up phone calls brought together focus groups for further discussion on the theme of remembering childhood media in China (conducted in Mandarin, Cantonese, and English). Two large evening and afternoon screenings of the films and animations recollected by the Beijing respondents were also arranged. These screenings were attended by over a hundred people (including their children) in each instance. All attendees filled out further questionnaires and younger children drew pictures of favourite characters. There was on-the-spot focus group follow-up with Mainland Chinese migrants who had brought their children to the screenings. Research assistants also carried out observations during screenings, and one was assigned to work with children whilst they were drawing to discuss their ideas. Drawing and screenings with the "Saturday morning" Chinese-language schools also led to a further thirty responses from teenagers, and to a television segment for Channel 31, "Chungwah," created by the children in the primary classes at Leeming. This interactive approach gave the researchers a good sense of how the films were received, and the inter-generational differences between sections of the audience.

Following analysis of this material, the research moved back to Beijing to conduct similar screenings and discussions with parents and focus groups in schools. The researcher took her own children with her and participated in many school and extracurricular activities, which deepened a quasi-ethnographic layer of observation, and also facilitated impromptu discussions with mothers (on school outings, at play-parks, in department stores, and so on), teachers, and other children. This work elicited a great deal of observational data, as well as a good sense of children's everyday media use.

In parallel to this strand of the work, formal interviews were again conducted with media workers, film scholars, and with senior members of the film world (from Xie Jin to Xie Tian). These were useful as they provided a historical depth to the understanding gained from less formal conversations. A great deal of time was spent locating and viewing children's films, many of which had not been given a VCD or video release. We also watched a lot of television!

A further dimension was added when educationalists asked the author to help produce a CD-ROM version of an English textbook series currently being trialed in Chinese primary schools. This allowed us to test the CD-ROM with students the following year, again with new migrants in WA and with school children in Beijing. Each child was given about an hour to work through the CD-ROM and was observed (and helped by the programmer if necessary). Usability and comprehension testing was then carried out with each child, who was also free to add comments on the concepts and images deployed in the program. Parents and grandparents were also invited in for evening meetings to view the program and offer comments on its value, and give us information on the computers to which they and the children had regular access.

In 2002, a final visit was made to Beijing, Zibo, and Shanghai. Before the visit, questionnaires had been distributed to schools across five provinces through the good offices of the Film Course (critiqued in this book), and also through schools previously canvassed in Beijing. This survey focused on children as creative consumers, asking them questions about their choices, their ideas, and their suggestions for new productions. These were also followed up by focus groups in Zibo and Beijing. Again, interviews with Studio personnel and directors, with bureaucrats and with scholars, were carried out to gain a production and institutional perspective on the findings. Again, too, observational data was collected at screenings, in homes, and in schools.

The approach has therefore been one that draws on the soft (qualitative) empiricism of social anthropology (Miller and Slater 2000), with some caveats due to the constrictions around child surveys in China (police clearance is a normal hurdle for work with children in Australia but that is compounded by the requirement in China that surveys have some domestic institutional partner, pragmatically a school or a children's media outlet in this instance). The research was fortunate to have partners at Tsinghua University, and the advice of many local researchers and academics. It is necessary to state, however, that the analyses of the materials presented here is entirely the view and responsibility of the present author. Where appropriate, and it is often so in the PRC, primary data from respondents has been given an institutional context. Textual analysis too relies on the author's reading of the political motivations of the state in China. None of the respondents should shoulder any responsibility for my errors or opinions.

Glossary of Chinese Terms

A Yao Lan 啊！摇篮

Bai Yi Zhan Shi 白衣战士

Bao Lian Deng 宝莲灯

Bie Ku Ma Ma 别哭妈妈

Cao Fang Zi 草房子

Cui Gang Hong Qi 翠岗红旗

Da Nao Tian Gong 大闹天宫

Da Qi Ceng Xiao Shi 大气层消失

Dai Dai Xiang Chuan 代代相传

Dian Ying Yi Shu Jia 电影艺术家

Dong Fang Ying Shi Fa Xing Gong Si 东方影视发行公司

Dong Hua Pian 动画片

Dui Hong Wei Bing Hong Xiao Bin Guang Bo 对红卫兵红小兵广播

Er Tong Jie Mu 儿童节目

Er Tong Le Yuan 儿童乐园

Er Tong Shi Dai 儿童时代

Er Tong Shi Jie 儿童世界

Fang Xi 放西

Feifei Cong Ying Ji 飞飞从影记

Feng Tu Zi 疯兔子

Feng Zheng　风筝

Gan Qing　感情

Ge Ming Jia Ting　革命家庭

Ge Ren Dao De　个人道德

Gu Er Jiu Zu Ji　孤儿救祖记

Gu Shi Da Wang　故事大王

Guang Bo Dian Ying Dian Shi Bu　广播电影电视部

Guo Jia　国家

Guo Min Dang　国民党

Hao Hai Zi　好孩子

Hao Peng You——Shu　好朋友——书

Hong Hai Zi　红孩子

Hong Xiang　红象

Hong Xiao Bing　红小兵

Hong Xiao Bing Yin Yue Wu Dao　红小兵音乐舞蹈

Hua Er Duo Duo　花儿朵朵

Hua Ji　花妓

Huan Bao Yi Shi　环保意识

Huo Yan Shan Lai De Gu Shou　火焰山来的鼓手

Ji Mao Xin　鸡毛信

Jia Ting Guan Xi　家庭关系

Jia You　加油

Jian Kang De Sheng Huo　健康的生活

Jian Zhi Pian　剪纸片

Jiao Yu　教育

Kan Zhuo Bie Lin　看卓别林

Ke Xue De Guan Li　科学的管理

Kong Bai　空白

Kuai Le Shao Nian　快乐少年

Lan Mao　蓝猫

Li Shi　历史

Lie Huo Zhong Yong Sheng　烈火中永生

Lin Jia Pu Zi　林家铺子

Liu Ge Yi Bai　六个一百

Long Xu Gou　龙须沟

Lu Bing Hua　鲁冰花

Meng Gu Min Zu　蒙古民族

Mi Tu De Gao Yang　迷途的羔羊

Miao Miao　苗苗

Min Zu Shi　民族史

Mo Fan　模范

Mu Ou Pian　木偶片

Ne Zha Nao Hai　哪咤闹海

Quan Dang Quan She Hui Dou Yao Guan Xin Shao Nian Er Tong De Jian Kang Cheng Zhang　全党全社会都要关心少年儿童的健康成长

Ren Lei Zhi You Yi Ge Di Qiu　人类只有一个地球

Ren Min Ri Bao　人民日报

Ren Yi Li Zhi Xin　仁、义、礼、智、信

San Ge He Shang　三个和尚

San Mao Cong Jun Ji　三毛从军记

Sanmao　三毛

Shan Shan De Hong Xing　闪闪的红星

Shanghai Za Zhi　上海杂志

Shao Nian Er Tong Jie Mu　少年儿童节目

Shao Nian Gong　少年宫

Shen Bi Ma Liang　神笔马良

Shi Zi Wang　狮子王

Si Ge Xiao Huo Ban　四个小伙伴

Su Xiaosan　苏小三

Su Zhi　素质

Sun Wukong　孙悟空

Ta Dui Ye Ye You Hen Shen De Gan Qing, Ye Ye Gen Ta Shuo, Ren Si Hou Hui Bian Cheng Yi Tiao Yu　他对爷爷有很深的感情，爷爷跟他说，人死后会变成一条鱼

Tai Tai　太太

Tian Tang Hui Xin　天堂回信

Ting Mao Zhu Xi Hua, Gen Gong Chan Dang Zou　听毛主席话，跟共产党走

Tong Nian Zai Ruijin　童年在瑞金

Tong Niu Jiang　童牛奖

Wai Guo　外国

Wan Tong　顽童

Wang Xiaomao　王小毛

Wen Hua　文化

Wo He Wo De Tong Xue　我和我的同学

Wo Men Zhi Shi Rang Hai Zi Men Zhi Dao　我们只是让孩子们知道

Wo Shi Yi Tiao Yu　我是一条鱼

Wu Dao　舞蹈

Wu Zhi Xiang Shou　物质享受

Xi Bo　锡伯

Xi You Ji　西游记

Xia Gang　下岗

Xia Hai　下海

Xiao Bin Zhang Ga　小兵张嘎

Xiao Hai Yue Bao　小孩月报

Xiao Ke Dou Zhao Ma Ma　小蝌蚪找妈妈

Xiao Ling Dang　小铃铛

Xiao Peng You　小朋友

Xiao Wai　校外

Xiao Wai Jiao Yu　校外教育

Xiao Xiao Ju Le Bu　小小俱乐部

Xiao Xiao Shi Jie　小小世界

Xiao Xue　小学

Xin Shao Nian　新少年

Xin Xue Nian Kai Shi Le　新学年开始了

Xing Wei Fang Shi　行为方式

Xue Nü Wang　雪女王

Ya Zhou　亚洲

Yang Qi Ni De Xiao Lian　仰起你的笑脸

Yi Bu Hao De Zuo Pin Chang Hui Ying Xiang Hai Zi De Yi Sheng　一部好的作品常会
影响孩子的一生

Yi Ge Ye Bu Neng Shao　一个也不能少

Yi Tiao Xian　一条线

You Mo Da Shi　幽默大师

Za Bao Zi 砸薄子

Zhan Guo 战国

Zhi Shi 知识

Zhong 忠

Zhong Gong Zhong Yang Xuan Chuan Bu 中共中央宣传部

Zhong Guo 中国

Zhong Guo Ai Zi Ying Shi Jiao Yu Cu Jin Hui 中国爱子影视教育促进会

Zhong Guo Bei Ju Lun Li Mo Shi 中国悲剧伦理模式

Zhong Guo Er Tong 中国儿童

Zhong Guo Er Tong Shao Nian Dian Ying Xue Hui 中国儿童少年电影学会

Zhong Guo Shao Nian Bao 中国少年报

Zhong Hua Min Zu Guo 中华民族国

Zhong Yang Dian Shi Tai 中央电视台

Zi You 自由

Zi Zhu He Can Yu 自主和参与

Zu Guo De Hua Duo 祖国的花朵

Selected Bibliography

Allen, S. L. 1994. *Media Anthropology: Informing Global Citizen.* Westport, Conn.: Bergin and Harvey.

Amory, A., et al. 1999. "The Use of Computer Games as an Educational Tool: Identification of Appropriate Games Types and Game Elements." *British Journal of Educational Technology* 30, no. 4: 311–21.

Anagnost, Ann. 1997. "Children and National Transcendence in China." In *Constructing China: The Interaction of Culture and Economics*, ed. K. Lieberthal, 195–221. Ann Arbor: Center for Chinese Studies, University of Michigan.

Anderson, James, ed. 2002. *Transnational Democracy: Political Spaces and Border Crossings.* London: Routledge.

Anstey, M., and G. Bull. 2000. *Reading the Visual.* New South Wales: Harcourt.

Arac, Jonathan. 1997. "Postmodernism and Postmodernity in China: An Agenda for Inquiry." *New Literary History* 28, no. 1:135–46.

Arendrup, Birthe, Carsten Boyer Thogersen, and Anne Wedell Wedellsborg, eds. 1986. *China in the 1980s and Beyond.* Richmond, Va.: Curzon Press.

Ashbach, Charles. 1994. "Media Influences and Personality Development: The Inner Image and the Outer World." *Media, Children, and the Family: Social Scientific, Psychodynamic, and Clinical Perspectives*, ed. Dolf Zillmann, Jennings Bryson, and Althea C. Huston, 117–38. Hillsdale, N.J.: Lawrence Erlbaum.

Baik, Young-seo. 2002. "Conceptualising 'Asia' in the Modern Chinese Mind: a Korean Perspective." *Inter-Asia Cultural Studies* 3, no. 2 (August): 277–86.

Balnaves, Mark, James Donald, and Stephanie H. Donald. 2002. *The Penguin Atlas of Media and Information.* New York: Penguin Books.

Barker, Martin, and Julian Petley. 1997. *Ill Effects: The Media/Violence Debate.* London: Routledge.

Barlow, Tani E., and Donald M. Lowe. 1987. *Teaching China's Lost Generation.* San Francisco: China Books.

Bazalgette, Carey, and David Buckingham. 1995. *In Front of the Children: Screen Entertainment and Young Audiences.* London: BFI.

Becker, Henry Jay. 2000. "Who's Wired and Who's Not: Children's Access to and Use of Computer Technology." *Children and Computer Technology* 10, no. 2: 44–74.

Beemer, Hartley L. 2001. "Educational Development in China's West." *Center for Chinese Education.* www.tc.columbia.edi/centers/coce/pdf-files/beemersummary.pdf (19 August 2001).

Behnke Kinney, Anne, ed. 1995. *Chinese Views of Childhood.* Honolulu: University of Hawaii Press.

Benewick, Robert, and Stephanie H. Donald. 2003. "Treasuring the Word: Mao, Depoliticisation, and the Material Present." *Asian Politics in Development: Essays in Honour of Gordon White,* ed. Robert Benewick, Marc Blecher, and Sarah Cook, 65–82. London: Frank Cass.

Berg, Gary A. 2000. "Human-computer Interaction (HCI) in Educational Environments: Implications of Understanding Computers as Media." *Journal of Educational Multimedia and Hypermedia* 9, no. 4: 349–70.

Bernstein, Basil. 2000. *Pedagogy, Symbolic Control and Identity: Theory, Research, Critique.* Lanham, Md.: Rowman & Littlefield.

Berry, Chris. 2002. "Facing Reality: Chinese Documentary, Chinese Postsocialism." *The First Guangzhou Triennial Reinterpretation: A Decade of Experimental Chinese Art (1990–2000),* ed. Wu Hung, 121–31. Guangdong Museum of Art. Chicago: Art Media Resources.

Biesenbach-Lucas, Sigrun, and Donald Weasenforth. 2001. "E-mail and Word Processing in the ESL Classroom: How the Medium Affects the Message." *Language, Learning and Technology* 5, no. 1: 135–45.

Bishop, Ana. 2001. "An Expert's Guide to Products for the Multilingual Classroom." *Technology and Learning* 21, no. 9: 39–47.

Blecher, Marc. 1997. *China against the Tides: Restructuring through Revolution, Radicalism and Reform.* London: Pinter.

Broughton, John M. 1985. "The Surrender of Control: Computer Literacy as Political Socialization of the Child." *The Computer in Education: A Critical Perspective,* ed. D. Sloan, 101–22. New York: Teachers College Press.

Buckingham, David. 1999. "Young People, Politics and News Media: Beyond Political Socialisation." *Oxford Review of Education* 25, no. 1/2: 171–84.

———. 2000. *After the Death of Childhood: Growing Up in the Age of Electronic Media.* Cambridge: Polity Press.

———. 2002. *Small Screens: Television for Children.* Leicester: Leicester University Press.

Burch, Noel. 1979. *To the Distant Observer: Form and Meaning in the Japanese Cinema.* London: Scolar.

Cahoon, Brad. 2000. "Electronic Literacies: Language, Culture, and Power in Online Education." *Journal of Higher Education* 71, no. 5: 627–29.

Caves, Richard E. 2000. *Creative Industries: Contracts between Art and Commerce.* Cambridge, Mass.: Harvard University Press.

Chao, Julie. 2002. "China Pushing Creativity, Rigid Schooling Stifles Progress." *Atlanta Journal* (May 12): B1.

Chen, Guangsheng. 1968. *Lei Feng: Chairman Mao's Good Fighter.* Beijing: Foreign Languages Press.

Cheng, K.-M., and K.-H. Wong. 2001. "China's Education System at a Glance up to 2001." *China Educational Forum* 3, no. 1. www.hku.hk/chinaed/newsletter/glance .html (16 November 2001).

China Teenage Research Institution. 2000. "A Report on Media and Contemporary Youth" (*Julang de chongji: meijie yu dangdai shaonian ertong*). In *New Discoveries: A Report on Contemporary Chinese Children and Youth* (*Xin faxian: dangdai zhongguo shaonian ertong baogao*). Beijing: China Children's Publishing House (*Zhongguo shaonian ertong chubanshe*).

Christiansen, Flemming. 2002. "Will WTO Accession Threaten China's Social Stability?" *China's Accession to the World Trade Organization*, ed. Heike Holbig and Robert Ash. London: Routledge Curzon.

Chu Yinghchi, Stephanie H. Donald, and Andrea Witcomb. 2003. "Children, Media, and the Public Sphere in Chinese Australia." *Political Communications in Greater China: The Construction and Reflection of Identity*, ed. Gary Rawnsley and Ming-yeh Rawnsley. London: Routledge Curzon.

Clark, Paul. 1989. *Chinese Cinema.* Cambridge: Cambridge University Press.

Cleverley, John. 1985. *The Schooling of China: Tradition and Modernity in Chinese Education.* Boston: Allen & Unwin.

Clifford, Barry R., B. Gunter, and J. McAleer. 1995. *Television and Children: Program Evaluation, Comprehension and Impact.* Hillsdale, N.J.: Lawrence Erlbaum.

Cope, Brian, and Mary Kalantzis. 2000. *Multiliteracies: Literacy Learning and the Design of Social Futures.* Victoria: Macmillan.

Cultural Revolution in China's Schools, May 1966–April 1969. 1988. Stanford, Calif.: Hoover Institution Press.

Curtis, Barry, 1995. "'In-Betweening': An Interview with Irene Kotlarz." *Art History* 18, no. 1: 24–36.

Dahlgren, Peter. 2002. "In Search of the Talkative Public: Media, Deliberative Democracy and Civic Culture." *Javnost/The Public: Journal of the European Institute for Communication and Culture* 9, no. 3: 5–26.

Davies, Gloria, ed. 2001. *Voicing Concerns: Contemporary Chinese Critical Inquiry.* Lanham, Md.: Rowman & Littlefield.

Davis, Darrell, and Steven Harrell. 1993. *Chinese Families in the Post-Mao Era.* Los Angeles: University of California Press.

Derrida, Jacques. 2001. *Cosmopolitanism and Forgiveness.* London: Routledge.

Dirlik, Arif, and Zahng Xudong, eds. 2000. *Postmodernism and China.* Durham, N.C.: Duke University Press.

Dittmer, Lowell. 1974. *Liu Shao-ch'i and the Chinese Cultural Revolution.* Berkeley: University of California Press.

Donald, Stephanie Hemelryk, and Ingrid Richardson. 2002. "The English Project: Function and Culture in New Media Research." *Inter/Sections: The Journal of Global Communications and Culture* 2, no. 5: 155–66.

Donald, Stephanie H., and Christina Lee. 2001. "Ambiguous Women in Contemporary Chinese Film." *Images of the "Modern Woman" in Asia: Global Media/Local Meanings*, ed. Shoma Munshi, 123–37. London: Curzon.

Donald, Stephanie. 1999. "Children as Political Messengers: Space and Aesthetics in Posters and Film." In *Picturing Power in the People's Republic of China: Posters of the Cultural Revolution*, ed. Harriet Evans and Stephanie Donald, 79–100. Lanham, Md.: Rowman & Littlefield.

———. 2000. *Public Secrets, Public Spaces: Cinema and Civility in China*, Lanham, Md.: Rowman & Littlefield.

———. 2002a. "Children's Day: The Fashionable Performance of Modern Citizenship in China." In *Fashioning the Body Politic: Dress, Gender, Citizenship*, ed. Wendy Parkins, 205–16. Oxford: Berg.

———. 2002b. "Crazy Rabbits! Children's Media Culture." *Media in China: Consumption, Content and Crisis*, ed. Stephanie H. Donald, Michael Keane, and Yin Hong, 128–38. London: Routledge Curzon.

Durrant, Cal, and Bill Green. 2000. "Literacy and the New Technologies in School Education: Meeting the L(IT)eracy Challenge?" *Australian Journal of Language and Literacy* 23, no. 2: 89–102.

Edgar, Patricia. 1977. *Children and Screen Violence*. St Lucia: University of Queensland Press.

———. 1983. *Children and Television: Policy Implications*. Melbourne: ACTF.

———. 1984. *Children's Television: The Case for Regulation*. Melbourne: ACTF.

Edgar, Patricia, and Ray Crooke. 1976. *Families without Television*. Bundoora: La Trobe University.

Education Law of the People's Republic of China (*Zhonghua Renmin Gong he Guo jiaoyu fa*). 1995. Beijing: China Legal Publishing House (*Zhongguo fazhi chubanshe*).

Evans, Harriet. 1997. *Women and Sexuality in China: Dominant Discourses of Female Sexuality and Gender since 1949*. Cambridge: Polity Press.

Farquhar, Mary Ann. 1999. *Children's Literature in China: from Lu Xun to Mao Zedon*. Armonk, N.Y.: M. E. Sharpe.

Feng, Ruyuan. 2001. *Zichuan Experimental Middle School: August 1994-April 2001* (*Zichuan shiyan zhongxue* 1994.8–2001.4). Zibo: Zibo Shandong, Zibo Sea and Sky Advertising Company (*Zibo Haitian Guanggao Zhiban Youxian Gongsi*).

Feng Guo. 2002. *Educational Century*, vol 3. Lide International Education Research Institute and Beijing Limai School, Beijing: Elephant Press.

Film Course in China: Special Issue for the Seventh (Zibo) International Children's Film Festival and International Symposium on Film Education for Middle School and Primary School. 2002. Beijing, Film Course Research Institute.

Friedman, Edward, Paul G. Pickowicz, and Mark Selden. 1991. *Chinese Village, Socialist State*. New Haven, Conn.: Yale University Press.

Fu, Poshek. 2003. *Between Shanghai and Hong Kong: The Politics of Chinese Cinemas*. Stanford: Stanford University Press.

Gao Fang. 2001. "National Style in Chinese Animation" (*Minzu fengge de tansuo: zhongguo donghua dianying*). *The Fictitious World: Looking for a Theory of Animation Film* (*Xuni de shijie: donghua dianying lilun tansuo*). Unpublished doctoral thesis.

Garton, J. 1997. "New Genres and New Literacies: The Challenge of the Virtual Curriculum." *Australian Journal of Language and Literacy* 20, no. 3: 209–22.

Garvie, Edie. 1976. *Breakthrough to Fluency: English as a Second Language for Young Children*. Oxford: Basil Blackwell.

Gauntlett, David. 1996. *Video Critical: Children, the Environment and Media Power.* Luton, U.K.: John Libby Media.

Get the Picture: Regulation of Commercial Free-to-Air Television Services. 2002. Australian Film Commission.

Giddens, Anthony. 1990. *The Consequences of Modernity,* Cambridge: Polity Press.

Giroux, Henry A. 1999. *The Mouse That Roared: Disney and the End of Innocence.* Lanham, Md.: Rowman & Littlefield.

Gladney, Dru C. 1994. "Representing Nationality in China: Refiguring Majority/ Minority Identities." *Journal of Asian Studies* 53, no. 1: 92–123.

Goodman, David, ed. 2004. *The Campaign to "Open Up the West": National, Provincial and Local Perspectives.* Cambridge: Cambridge University Press.

Goonasekera, Anura. 2001. *Children in the News: Reporting of Children's Issues in Television and the Press in Asia.* Singapore: Asian Media Information and Communication Centre and School of Communication Studies, Nanyang Technological University.

Goonasekera, Anura, et al. 2000. *Growing Up with TV: Asian Children's Experience.* Singapore: Asian Media Information and Communication Centre.

Greenhalgh, Susan. 1993. "The Peasantization of the One-Child Policy in Shaanxi." *Chinese Families in the Post-Mao Era,* ed. Deborah Davis and Steven Harrell, 219–50. Berkeley: University of California Press.

Griffiths, Merris, Jude Collins, Elise Seip Tonnessen, Ann-Marie Barry, and Helen Yeates. 1992. "Who's Afraid of the Big Bad Box? Children and TV Advertising in Four Countries: A Review." *Educational Media International* 29, no. 4: 254–60.

Gu, Mingyuan. 2001. "The Spirit of Curriculum Reform in Mainland China." *Educational Century (Jiaoyu Shiji)* 3: 21–23.

Guntarto, B. 2001. "Internet and the New Media: Challenge for Indonesian Children." *Media Asia* 28, no. 4: 195–203.

Guo, Dongjin, and Jing Zhang. 2002. *Typical Film Lesson Research:* Gulliver's Travels (*Zhuti keli yanjiu: Geliefu Luji*). Shenzhen: Shenzhen Nanshan Foreign Language School Film Study Group (*Shenzhen shi Nanshan dui guoyu xuexiao keti zu*), school pamphlet.

Han, Dongping. 2001. "Impact of the Cultural Revolution on Rural Education and Economic Development: The Case of Jimo County." *Modern China* 27, no. 1: 59–90.

Hansen, M. H. 1999. *Lessons in Being Chinese: Minority Education and Ethnic Identity in Southwest China.* Seattle: University of Washington Press.

Hartley, John. 1998. "When Your Child Grows Up Too Fast: Juvenation and the Boundaries of the Social in News Media." *Continuum Journal of Media and Cultural Studies* 12, no. 1: 9–22.

Hayhoe, Ruth. 1989. *China's Universities and the Open Door.* Armonk, N.Y.: M. E. Sharpe.

———, ed. 1992. *Education and Modernization: The Chinese Experience.* New York: Pergamon Press.

Hayhoe, Ruth, and M. Bastid, eds. 1987. *China's Education and the Industrialized World: Studies in Cultural Transfer.* Armonk, N.Y.: M. E. Sharpe.

Hein, Laura, and Mark Selden, eds. 2000. *Censoring History: Citizenship and Memory in Japan, Germany and the United States.* Armonk, N.Y.: M.E. Sharpe.

Hodge, Bob, and David Tripp. 1986. *Children and Television: A Semiotic Approach.* Cambridge: Polity Press.

Howells, J. 1998. "Innovation and Technology Transfer within Multinational Firms." In *Globalization, Growth and Governance: Creating an Innovative Economy*, ed. J. Michie, 50–70. Oxford: Oxford University Press.

Huang, Yufu, et al. 2000. (Chinese Academy of Social Sciences Team). "An Assessment of Children's TV Programmes in the People's Republic of China." In *Growing Up with TV*, ed. Anura Goonasekera et al., 12–47. Singapore: Asian Media Information and Communication Centre.

Huang, Yufu, Ning Liu, and Shi Ying. 2001. "Portrayal of Children in the News: A Case Study in China." *Children in the News*, ed. Anura Goonasekera, 47–64. Singapore: Asian Media Information and Communication Centre and School of Communication Studies, Nanyang Technological University.

Huston, Althea C., Dolf Zillman, and Jennings Bryant. 1994. "Media Influence, Public Policy, and the Family." *Media, Children and the Family: Social Scientific, Psychodynamic and Clinical Perspectives*, ed. Dolf Zillman, Bryant Jennings, and Althea C. Huston, 3–18. Hillsdale, N.J.: Erlbaum.

Ichilov, O., ed. 1990. *Political Socialization, Citizenship Education, and Democracy.* New York: Teachers' College Press.

Identifying Opportunities for Educational Cooperation with China: The Importance of Understanding China's Educational Needs. 2002. Chinalink: Educational Exchange and Consulting.

Ip, Yung-hok. 1997. "Politics and Individuality in Communist Revolutionary Culture." *Modern China* 23, no. 1: 33–68.

The International Symposium on Primary and Secondary School's Movie and TV Education: A Collection of Prize Winning Essays (Zhong xiaoxue yingshi jiaoyu guoji yan tao hui zuwei hui: Huojiang lun wenji). 2002. Beijing.

Jenkins, Henry, ed. 1998. *The Children's Culture Reader.* New York: New York University Press.

Jiang Yarong, and David Ashley. 2000. *Mao's Children in the New China: Voices from the Red Guard Generation.* London: Routledge.

Kapur, Jyotsna. 1999. "Out of Control: Television and the Transformation of Childhood in Late Capitalism." *Kids' Media Culture*, ed. Marsha Kinder, 122–36. Durham, N.C.: Duke University Press.

Keane, Michael. 2001. "Redefining Chinese Citizenship." *Economy and Society* 30, no. 1: 1–17.

———. 2003. "Civil Society, Regulatory Space and Cultural Authority in China's Television Industry." *Television, Regulation and Civil Society in Asia*, ed. Philip Kitley, 169–87. London: Routledge Curzon.

Khan, Azizur Rahman, and Carl Riskin. 2001. *Inequality and Poverty in China in the Age of Globalization.* Oxford: Oxford University Press.

Kinder, Marsha, ed. 1998. *Kids' Media Culture.* Durham, N.C.: Duke University Press.

Kline, Stephen. 1993. *Out of the Garden: Toys, TV and Children's Culture in the Age of Marketing.* London: Verso.

Komolsevin, Rosechongporn. 2002. "Education, Encouragement, Self-regulation: Children and the Internet in Thailand." *Kids On-line: Promoting Responsible Use and a Safe Environment on the Net in Asia*, ed. K. Shetty, 154–85. Singapore: Asian

Media Information and Communication Centre and School of Communication and Information, Nanyang Technological University.

Korhonen, Pekka. 2002. "Asia's Chinese Name." *Inter-Asia Cultural Studies* 3, no. 2 (August): 253–70.

Kwong, J. 1979. *Chinese Education in Transition: Prelude to the Cultural Revolution*. Montreal: McGill-Queen's University Press.

Laing, Ellen J. 1996. "Auspicious Images of Children in China: Ninth to Thirteenth Century." *Orientations* 27, no. 1 (January): 47–52.

Landsberger, Stefan. 1995. *Chinese Propaganda Posters*. Amsterdam: Pepin Press.

Lankshear, Colin, et al. 1997. *Changing Literacies*. Milton Keynes: Open University Press.

Lardy, Nicholas R. 2002. *Integrating China into the Global Economy*. Washington, D.C.: Brookings Institution Press.

Law, Wing Wah. 2000. "Education Legislation in the People's Republic of China." *Centre of Research on Education in China Quarterly Newsletter*. University of Sydney, 1–2.

Learn from the Good Model Lei Feng. 1990. Beijing: Xinhua Bookstore Press.

"Learning by What Example? Educational Propaganda in Twenty-First Century China." *Critical Asian Studies* 33, no. 4 (2001): 541–71.

Lee, Chin-Chuan, ed. 2000. *Power, Money and the Media: Communication Patterns and Bureaucratic Control in Cultural China*. Evanston, Ill.: Northwestern University Press.

Lee, Gerald B. 1987. *Values, Tradition and Social Change: A Study of School Textbooks in Taiwan and China*. Los Angeles: University of California.

Lee, Gregory B. 2003. "Re-taking Tiger Mountain by Television: Televisual Socialisation of the Contemporary Chinese Consumer." *Chinas Unlimited: Making the Imaginaries of China and Chineseness*, ed. Gregory Lee, 55–78. London: Routledge Curzon.

Lee, S. P. 2001. "Satellite Television and Chinese Migrants in Britain." *Media and Migration: Constructions of Mobility and Difference*, ed. Nancy Wood and Russell King, 143–57. London: Routledge.

Lee, Wing On, and G. A. Postiglione. 1995. *Social Change and Educational Development: Mainland China, Taiwan and Hong Kong*. Hong Kong: Centre of Asian Studies, University of Hong Kong.

Lei, Feng. 1990. *The Diary of Lei Feng*. Beijing: Liberation Army Art and Literature Press.

Li, Haibo. 2002. "No More Carefree Childhood." *Beijing Review* 45, no. 31: 7.

Liao, Ping-Hui. 2001. "Love, Hope and Shopping: Decoding Advertisements in the Taipei MRT." Paper presented at Transnational Advertising in Asia Conference, sponsored by the Transnational China Project, Rice University, and the Center for the Study of Globalization and Cultures, University of Hong Kong, Hong Kong, 5 March.

Light, Paul, and Karen Littleton. 1999. *Social Processes in Children's Learning*. Cambridge: Cambridge University Press.

Limai School. 2002. "China after WTO: An Urgent Demand for a Significant Development of Vocational Technical Education—On the Basic Strategy to Change the Less-Developed Conditions of China's Vocational Technical Education" (*jiaru*

WTO de zhongguo: yuying zhiye, jishu jiaoyu de da fazhan). *Educational Century* (*jiaoyu shi ji wencong*) 3: 6–18.

Lin, A-Mien. 2001. *Origins of Children's Film* (*Mu hou geng yun jie shuo guo: de tou ertong dianying bie ben ji*). Beijing: China Film Development Press.

Lin, Jing. 1993. *Education in Post-Mao China*. Westport, Conn.: Praeger.

———. 1999. *Social Transformation and Private Education in China*. New York: Greenwood.

Link, Perry, and Kate Zhou. 2002. "*Shunkouliu:* Popular Satirical Sayings and Popular Thought." *Popular China: Unofficial Culture in a Globalizing Society*, ed. Perry Link, Richard P. Madsen, and Paul G. Pickowicz, 89–110. Lanham, Md.: Rowman & Littlefield.

Litzinger, Ralph A. 1995. "Making Histories: Contending Conceptions of the Yao Past." *Cultural Encounters on China's Ethnic Frontiers*, ed. Steven Harrell, 117–39. Washington: University of Washington Press.

Liu, Kang. 2004. "Is There an Alternative to (Capitalist) Globalization? The Debate about Modernity, Postmodernity, and Postcoloniality." *Globalization and Cultural Trends in China*, 23–45. Honolulu: University of Hawai'i Press.

Livingstone, Sonia. 2002. *Young People and New Media: Childhood and the Changing Media Environment*. London: Sage.

Lull, James. 1990. *China Turned On: Television, Reform, and Resistance*. London: Routledge.

Lynch, Daniel C. 1999. *After the Propaganda State: Media, Politics and "Thought Work" in Reformed China*. Stanford, Calif.: Stanford University Press.

Ma, Eric Kit-wai. 2001. "Consuming Satellite Modernities." *Cultural Studies* 3–4: 444–63.

Ma, Jinke. 1995. "The Social Role and Function of Examination as Seen from the Reform of China's University Entrance Examination." *Social Change and Educational Development*, ed. Gerald Postiglione, 290–97. Centre of Asian Studies Occasional Papers and Monographs no. 115. Hong Kong: University of Hong Kong, Centre of Asian Studies.

Mab Huang. 2000. "Universal Human Rights and Chinese Liberalism." *Human Rights and Asian Values: Contesting National Identities and Cultural Representations in Asia*, ed. Michael Jacobsen and Ole Brun, 227–48. London: Curzon.

Macklin, C. M., and L. Carlson, eds. 1999. *Advertising to Children: Concepts and Controversies*. London: Sage.

Matthews, B. M. 2000. "The Chinese Value Survey: An Interpretation of Value Scales and Consideration of Some Preliminary Results." *International Journal of Education Journal* 1, no. 2: 117–27.

Miller, Toby, Nitin Govil, John McMurria, and Richard Maxwell. 2001. *Global Hollywood*. London: BFI.

Miller, Daniel, and Don Slater. 2000. *The Internet: An Ethnographic Approach*. Oxford: Berg.

Morris, Andrew. 2002. "'I Believe You Can Fly': Basketball Culture in Postsocialist China." *Popular China: Unofficial Culture in a Globalizing Society*, ed. Perry Link, Richard P. Madsen, and Paul G. Pickowicz, 9–38. Lanham, Md.: Rowman & Littlefield.

Mouffe, Chantal. 2000. *The Democratic Paradox*. London: Verso.

National Report on Film and Television Education for Primary and High School Students (Quanguo zhong xiao xuesheng ying shi jiaoyu tongxun). 2002. Beijing: Audio-Visual Committee of the Ministry of Education.

Newman, Michael. 2002. "Reconceptualising Democracy in the European Union." *Transnational Democracy: Political Spaces and Border Crossing*, ed. James Andersen, 73–92. London: Routledge.

New Student Enrolment by Level and Type of School. 2002. China: Education and Research Network. www.edu.cn (19 September).

Ni Zhen. 2002. *Memoirs from the Beijing Film Academy: The Genesis of China's Fifth Generation*, trans. Chris Berry. Durham, N.C.: Duke University Press.

Number of Schools by Level and Type. 2002. China Education and Research Network. www.edu.cn (19 September).

Number of Student Enrolment by Level and Type of School. 2002. China Education and Research Network. www.edu.cn (19 September).

Oswell, David. 2002. *Television, Childhood and the Home: A History of the Making of the Child Television Audience in Britain*. Oxford: Oxford University Press.

Pecora, Nancy Odom. 1998. *The Business of Children's Entertainment*. London: Guilford.

Pepper, Suzanne. 1996. *Radicalism and Education Reform in Twentieth Century China: The Search for an Ideal Development Model*. Cambridge: Cambridge University Press.

Pheng Cheah and Bruce Robbins, eds. 1998. *Cosmopolitics: Thinking and Feeling Beyond the Nation*. Minneapolis: University of Minnesota Press.

Pijl, Kees van der. 2002. "Holding the Middle Ground in the Transnationalisation Process." *Transnational Democracy: Political Spaces and Border Crossings*, ed. James Andersen, 171–95. London: Routledge.

Postiglione, Gerald A., and Wing-On Lee, eds. 1995. *Social Change and Educational Development: Mainland China, Taiwan and Hong Kong*. Centre of Asian Studies Occasional Papers and Monographs no. 115. Hong Kong: University of Hong Kong, Centre of Asian Studies.

Pullman, Philip. 1995. *Northern Lights*. Part One of *His Dark Materials*. London: Scholastic Books.

Pye, Lucian W., with Mary W. Pye. 1985. *Asian Power and Politics: The Cultural Dimensions of Authority*. Cambridge, Mass.: Belknap Press of Harvard University Press.

Rawls, John. 1997. "The Idea of Public Reason." *Deliberative Democracy, Essays on Reason and Politics*, ed. J. Bohman and W. Rehg, 93–130. Cambridge, Mass.: Massachusetts Institute of Technology.

Read, Herbert. 1935/1968. *The Green Child*. London: Penguin Books.

Reuven, K., and T. Rapoport. 1990. "Informal Youth Movements and the Generation of Democratic Experience: An Israeli Example." *Political Socialisation*, ed. O. Ichilov, 221–39. New York: Teachers College Press.

Rifkin, J. 2000. *The Age of Access: How the Shift from Ownership to Access Is Transforming Capitalism*. London: Penguin Books.

Robbins, Bruce. 1998a. "Actually Existing Cosmopolitanism." *Cosmopolitics*, ed. Pheng Cheah and Bruce Robbins, 1–19. Minneapolis: University of Minnesota Press.

———. 1998b. "Comparative Cosmopolitanisms." *Cosmopolitics*, ed. Pheng Cheah and Bruce Robbins, 246–64. Minneapolis: University of Minnesota Press.

Rodan, Garry. 1996. "The Internationalisation of Ideological Conflict: Asia's New Significance." *The Pacific Review* 9, no. 3: 328–51.

Rosen, Stanley. 1992. "Women, Education and Modernisation." *Education and Modernization*, ed. Ruth Hayhoe, 255–84. New York: Pergamon Press.

———. 1995. "Women and Reform in China." *Social Change and Educational Development*, ed. Gerald Postiglione, 130–38. Hong Kong: Centre of Asian Studies.

Sayers, Jane, and Eva Sternfeld. 2001. "Environmental Education in China." *Berliner China-Hefte* 21: 42–55.

Schlesinger, Philip. 1991. *Media, State and Nation: Political Violence and Collective Identities*. London: Sage.

Shi, Jinghuan. 1995. "China's Cultural Tradition and Women's Participation in Education." *Social Change and Educational Development*, ed. Gerald Postiglione, 139–49. Hong Kong: Centre of Asian Studies, University of Hong Kong.

Shi Jiannong, Lei Zhenxiao, and Wang Liuyi. 2002. "Movie and Child Development." In *Film Course in China*, trans. Li Ling, 6–11. Beijing: Film Course Research Team Publication.

Silverblatt, A. 1995. *Media Literacy: Key to Interpreting Media Messages*. Westport, Conn.: Praeger.

Smoodin, Eric. 1993. *Animating Culture: Hollywood Cartoons from the Sound Era*. New Brunswick, N.J.: Rutgers University Press.

———, ed. 1994. *Disney Discourse: Producing the Magic Kingdom*. London: Routledge.

Soysal, Y. N. 2000. "Identity and Transnationalization in German School Textbooks." In *Censoring History: Citizenship and Memory in Japan, Germany and the United States*, ed. Laura Hein and Mark Selden, 127–49. Armonk, N.Y.: M. E. Sharpe.

Spivak, Gayatri C. 1998. "Cultural Talks in the Hot Peace: Revisiting the 'Global Village.'" In *Cosmopolitics*, ed. Pheng Cheah and Bruce Robbins, 329–50. Minneapolis: University of Minnesota Press.

State Education Commission Education in China, 1978–1988. 1989. Beijing: State Education Commission.

Strasburger, V. C., and B. J. Wilson (with J. Funk, E. Donnerstein, and B. McCannon). 2002. *Children, Adolescents and the Media*. London: Sage.

Sun, Wanning. 2002. *Leaving China: Media, Migration and Transnational Imagination*. Lanham, Md.: Rowman & Littlefield.

Tai, Y. Q. 1990. *Allow Children to be Happier*. Beijing: China Film Publisher.

Tang, Qingyuan. 2002. *Motion Pictures and Environmental Protection* (*Dianying yu huan bao*). Pingxiang, Jiangxi, Pingxiang Experimental Kindergarten (*Jiangxi Pingxiang shi shiyan you'er yuan*).

Tang, W. F., and W. L. Parish. 2000. *Chinese Urban Life under Reform: The Changing Social Contract*. Cambridge: Cambridge University Press.

Ting. 1998. *An Analysis and Discussion of Children's Film Theories*, vol 2. Beijing: China Peace Publisher.

Tripp, Robert, and David Tripp. 1986. *Children and Television: A Semiotic Approach*. Cambridge: Polity Press.

Tsang, Mun C. 2001. "Intergovernmental Grants and the Financing of Compulsory Education in China." published online, Columbia Center for Chinese Education. www.tc.columbia.edu/centers/coce/ (15 September).

Unesco. 2002. *Education for All: Global Monitoring Report, Is the World on Track?* Paris: Unesco Publishing IIEP.

———. 2003. *Literacy Skills for the World of Tomorrow: Further Results from PISA.* Paris: Unesco Publishing IIEP.

Unesco (David P. Weikart). 2000. *Early Childhood Education: Need and Opportunity.* Paris: Unesco Publishing IIEP.

Walkerdine, Valerie. 1984. "Developmental Psychology and the Child-Centred Pedagogy: The Insertion of Piaget into Early Education." *Changing the Subject: Psychology, Social Regulation and Subjectivity,* ed. Julian Henriques, Wendy Holloway, Cathy Urwin, Couze Venn, and Valerie Walkerdine. London: Cambridge University Press.

———. 1989. *The Mastery of Reason: Cognitive Development and the Production of Rationality.* London: Cambridge University Press.

Wang, Aimin. 2002. "Validation of a Self-Control Rating Scale in a Chinese Pre-School." *Journal of Research in Childhood Education* 16, no. 2 (Spring): 189–201.

Wang, L., and L. Li. 2000. *Film Course in China.* Beijing: China.

Wang, Jing. 2001. "'Culture' as Leisure and 'Culture' as Capital." *Positions: East Asia Cultures Critique* 9, no. 1:68–104.

———. 2004. "The Global Reach of a New Discourse." *International Journal of Cultural Studies* 7, no. 1:9–20.

Waniganayake, M., and B. Donegan. 1999. "Political Socialisation During Early Childhood." *Australia Journal of Early Childhood* 24, no. 1: 34–42.

Wartella Ellen, ed. 1979. *Children Communicating: Media and Development of Thought, Speech, Understanding.* California: Sage.

———. 2002. "New Directions in Media Research and Media Effects on Children." Keynote address, Australian Symposium on "The Eyes of the Child: The World They'll See in the Twenty-First Century." Melbourne.

Watson, James L. 1997. *Golden Arches East.* Stanford, Calif.: Stanford University Press.

Willis, Susan. 1999. *Inside the Mouse.* Lanham, Md.: Rowman & Littlefield.

Wu, Chih-hsien. 1998. *Children and Television (Ertong yu dianshe).* Taibei: Jiayun Publishing.

———. 2001. "A Content Analysis of Alcohol Advertising on Taiwanese Television and Effects of Media Literacy on Elementary Children's Opinions of Alcohol and Drinking." Working paper. Taibei: National Tainan Teachers' College.

———. 2002a. "A Study of the Phenomenon of Young Children's Consumption of Popular Japanese Cartoon Products." *Modern Education Monthly* 43, no. 6: 13–25.

———. 2002b. "The Study of Children's Consumption of Popular Japanese Cartoon Products." *Social Education* 43, no. 6: 13–25.

Wu Chih-hsien, and Chou Hui-mei. 2000. "A Study of the Television Literacy Program for Elementary School Children 1–11." *Social Education* 42, no. 2: 13–25.

Wu Pei-Yu. 1995. "Childhood Remembered: Parents and Children in China, 800–1700." *Chinese Views of Childhood,* ed. Anne Behnke Kinney, 129–56. Honolulu: University of Hawaii Press.

Xi, Jieying. 2000. *Annals of Chinese Children in the Twentieth Century (baininan zhongguo ertong).* Guangzhou: Xinshiji chubanshe.

Yang, Dongping. 2000a. *Education Evolution in China (III): Problems and Arguments.* China Education and Research Network. www.edu.cn/-20010101/22292.shtml (19 September).

———. 2000b. *Educational Evolution in China (I): Educational Evolution and Reform*, China Education and Research Network. www.edu.cn/20010101/-/22290 .shtml (19 September).

Yau, Esther Ching-mei. 1990. *Filmic Discourses on Women in Chinese Cinema (1949–1965): Art, Ideology, and Social Relations.* Ph.D. dissertation. Los Angeles: University of California.

Yogev, Abraham, and Rina Shapira. 1990. "Citizenship Socialisation in National Voluntary Youth Organisations." *Political Socialization*, ed. O. Ichilov, 205–20. New York: Teachers College Press.

Yu, X. 2001. "To Be a Child or Not?" (*hai ertong bu ertong le?*). *Life-Weekly* (*Sanlian shenghuo zhoukan*). Bookshop to Life Reading and New Knowledge (*Shenghuo dushu xinzhi sanlian shudian*) Issue 6–7 (February 11–18): 10–13.

Zelizer, Viviana A. 1998. "From Useful to Useless: Moral Conflict over Child Labour." *The Children's Culture Reader*, ed. Henry Jenkins, 81–94. New York: New York University Press.

Zhang, Yanbing, and Jake Harwood. 2002. "Television Viewing and Perceptions of Traditional Chinese Values among Chinese College Students." *Journal of Broadcasting and Electronic Media* 46, no. 2 (June): 245–65.

Zhao Bin and Graham Murdock. 1996. "Young Pioneers: Children and the Making of China Consumerism." *Cultural Studies* 10, no. 2.

Zhao Yuezhi. 1998. *Media, Market, and Democracy in China*. Urbana: University of Illinois Press.

Zheng Zhenqin. 1999. "A Complete Account of Children's Film." (*Buduan chengzhang de xinshiqi ertong dianying chuangzuo*). *Contemporary Movies* (*Dangdai dianying*), no. 5: 14–28.

Zhong Yong. 2003. "In Search of Loyal Audiences—What Did I Find? An Ethnographic Study of Chinese Television Audiences." *Continuum: Journal of Media and Cultural Studies* 17, no. 3: 233–46.

Zhou Nanzhao and Zhang Xuezhong. 2001. *Dictionary of Education* Beijing: Science Education Press.

Zhu, Weizheng. 1992. "Confucius and Traditional Chinese Education: An Assessment." *Education and Modernization*, ed. Ruth Hayhoe, 3–22. New York: Pergamon Press.

Zillman, Dolf, Jennings Bryant, and Althea C. Huston. 1984. *Media, Children and the Family: Social Scientific, Psychodynamic and Clinical Perspectives*. Hillsdale, N.J.: Erlbaum.

Index

access. *See* distribution; rural children
adult needs, 24. *See also* childhood;
    nostalgia
advertising, 17, 58–59
agency, 3, 6, 8, 42, 63, 65–71. *See also*
    competency; literacy
American media, 11; Chinese attitudes
    towards, 10–11, 66. *See also* Chaplin,
    Charlie; Disney
animation, 96–105; Chinese, 11–12, 14,
    16, 20n4, 30, 38, 63, 89, 96–105;
    Japanese, 3, 5, 10–12, 16, 54, 59, 66,
    72, 83, 89; South Korean, 25. *See also*
    American media, Chinese attitudes
    towards; Disney
Asian values, 76. *See also* Confucian
    values
atmosphere, 31

Baseball Boy, 49–50, 52, 54, 61
Beijing, 17, 94–96; media penetration in
    the district of, *94*
Beijing Film Academy, 1, 12, 33
Beijing Film Studios, 39, 45
Beijing Television, 15–17, 38–39
The Blue Kite, 39, 41

cartoons. *See* animation
CCP. *See* Chinese Communist Party
CCTV. *See* Chinese Central Television
celebrity, 16, 87
Chaplin, Charlie, 35–38, 90
childhood: adult ideals of, 24, 56–57;
    capital value of, 79–80; fantasies of,
    8, 25, 56; and labour, 57–59, 76–77;
    memories of, 6–7, 25, 41–43. *See also*
    education, pressures upon children
    of; nostalgia
Children's Day, 14, 38, 51–56
Children's Film Studio, 12, 15, 19,
    21–23, 26–31, 39, 41, 44–47, 63
children's media communications
    studies, ix–x, 1–8, 59–60
China Children's Film Society, 22, 31,
    39, 62, 68
China Daily, 52
China's Film Program. *See* Film Course
Chinese Central Television (CCTV), 5,
    15–16, 38, 45; Chinese Central
    Television 6 (CCTV6), 7, 13, 15, 46,
    106
Chinese Communist Party (CCP), 22–23,
    68

135

About the Author

Stephanie Hemelryk Donald is professor of communication and culture and director of the Research Centre in Trans/forming Cultures at the University of Technology, Sydney. She is the author of *Public Secrets, Public Spaces: Cinema and Civility in China*; coauthor of *The State of China Atlas* and *The State of Media and Information*; and coeditor of *Belief in China: Art, Deities, and Mortality*; *Media in China: Content, Consumption, and Crisis*; and *Picturing Power in the People's Republic of China: Posters of the Cultural Revolution*. She lives in Sydney with her family, James, Morag, and Ellen.